THE RIGHT TO BE NUBA

The Story of a Sudanese People's Struggle for Survival

Suleiman Musa Rahhal

International Nuba Coordination Centre

The Red Sea Press, Inc.
Publishers & Distributors of Third World Books

11-D Princess Road
Lawrenceville, NJ 08648

P. O. Box 48
Asmara, ERITREA

The Red Sea Press, Inc.
Publishers & Distributors of Third World Books

11-D Princess Road   P. O. Box 48
Lawrenceville, NJ 08648   Asmara, ERITREA

Copyright © 2001 International Nuba Coordination Centre

First Red Sea Press, Inc. Edition 2001

All rights reserved. No part of this publication may be reproduced, stored in a retrieval system or transmitted in any form or by any means electronic, mechanical, photocopying, recording or otherwise without the prior written permission of the publisher.

Cover Design: Debbie Hird
Cover photographs by George Rodger © 1949
  courtesy of the George Rodger Estate

Library of Congress Cataloging-in-Publication Data
The right to be Nuba : the story of a Sudanese people's struggle for survival / International Nuba Coordination Centre.
    p . cm.
Includes bibliographical references and index.
    ISBN 1-56902-136-8 -- ISBN 1-56902-137-6 (pbk.)
  1. Nuba (African people) --Social life and customs. 2. Nuba (African people) --Social conditions. 3. Sudan--politics and government--1985-
4. Nuba Mountains Region (Sudan)--politics and government. 5. Guerilla warfare--Sudan. I. International Nuba Coordination Centre (Organization)
    DT155.2.N82 R56 2000
    305.892'7624--dc21
                                                          00-010067

Contents

Foreword
    Suleiman Musa Rahhal — v

Glossary — viii

1. **The Right to be Nuba**
   Alex de Waal — 1

2. **The Nuba**
   Ahmed Abdel Rahman Saeed — 6

3. **The Nuba of South Kordofan**
   George Rodger — 21

4. **"Things Were No Longer the Same"**
   Yousif Kuwa Mekki — 25

5. **Focus on Crisis in the Nuba Mountains**
   Suleiman Musa Rahhal — 36

6. **The State of Sudan Today**
   Peter Woodward — 56

7. **Voices from the Nuba Mountains** — 59

8. **The Survival of the Nuba**
   David Stewart-Smith — 85

9.	The Nub Relief, Rehabilitation and Development Organisation *Neroun Phillip Kuku*	89
10.	Nuba Agriculture, Poverty or Plenty? *Ian Mackie*	99
11.	Democracy under Fire in the Nuba Mountains *Julie Flint*	103
12.	Unity in Diversity: Is it Possible in Sudan? *Ahmed Ibrahim Diraige*	113
13.	What Peace for the Nuba? *Suleiman Musa Rahhal*	115

Photographs between pages 24-25 and 88-89

Appendix 1: Clarifications on SPLM Peace Terms	121
Appendix 2: Resolutions of 1996 Conference	124
Appendix 3: List of the Disappeared and Killed	127
Information on Contributors	134
Information about the International Nuba Coordination Centre	136

Foreword

Suleiman Musa Rahhal

My former headmaster, the scholar and linguist Professor Roland Stevenson, who helped to record the grammar and vocabulary of the Nuba languages, once described the Nuba as a "vigorous hill people of good physique, much independence of mind, strong in traditions and fighting qualities." It is a fascinating remark that was made by someone who lived most of his life in the Nuba Mountains. I am proud to be one of these same Nuba people. It is for this reason I took up my pen to defend the collective rights of our remarkable people, to defend the right to be Nuba in the Sudan.

It is surprising how an individual can quickly be influenced by events and how quickly their course of life can also be changed. A little more than a decade ago the words "human rights" were not in my vocabulary and hardly crossed my mind, although I knew something about human rights from the Helsinki Conference in 1975. Perhaps my scanty knowledge and lack of interest in the concept and the philosophy of human rights at the beginning was due to the fact that my mind at that time was occupied with other things including my work as a senior scientific officer in the Department of Virology at St. Mary's Hospital, London.

It was only in early 1990 when I received sad news from my hometown Kadugli, which revealed systematic killing and disappearance of educated young Nuba and community leaders in Kadugli, that my life began to take its new direction. Among the "disappeared" many were relatives. I became sadder and more worried when I learned that my relatives including my cousin Mohammed Nowar, who was very close to me from childhood, were among those killed in cold blood. Horrific stories were filtering through as well, which revealed the upsurge in systematic violence that turned into a campaign of ethnic cleansing. Massacres had taken place in Lagowa and Logori areas, and many dead bodies were found scattered in the farms and the bushes. People were taken from their homes and offices and never returned. No one knows their whereabouts. A terrible situation that reflected a curfew developed in the whole region and all people became frightened. It became clear that the Nuba had been targeted by the NIF regime, because of their cultural identity. All these abuses were committed against the Nuba with complete impunity. And at this stage there was no news or report at all on these grave crimes.

It was for this reason I said to myself "something must be done" to protect these innocent people before they were all wiped out. Indeed, I decided to join the human rights movement to become an activist myself, to defend the collective rights of my people. I then joined the struggle.

I am glad that the hard work of Nuba Mountains Solidarity Abroad and international human rights organisations has paid off and made a profound impact to bring to light human rights abuses in the Nuba Mountains. The systematic genocidal campaign by the government seems to have abated now and the plight for the Nuba people has gained recognition by the international community.

The purpose of this book is to draw the attention to the Nuba predicament and to the plight of the Nuba in Southern Kordofan. The Nuba Mountains region has been sealed off from the outside world for most of the past twelve years. Humanitarian aid agencies were forbidden to enter the area, and for many years the struggle of the Nuba people seemed to have been forgotten. The NIF regime has been using food as a weapon of war in order to starve the Nuba to submission. The government has been forcing them to "peace villages" which are like concentration camps, where women are raped, youths are forced to join the Popular Defence Forces and fight their own people, and older men and women are used as unpaid labour in agricultural farms owned by rich and powerful merchants and army officers from Khartoum.

This book has contributions that deal with the human rights crisis in the Nuba Mountains and also covers aspects of Nuba history, culture, and political future in Sudan. It has testimonies from Nuba themselves, describing their suffering, their resistance, and their political and humanitarian work.

The Right to be Nuba is also a book that illustrates the diversity of Nuba cultures, languages and religions which had made Nuba unique and different from their Arab neighbours and other Sudanese people. *The Right to be Nuba* contains articles written and pictures taken by the famous photographer George Rodger, that were taken in the Nuba Mountains in 1948. These magnificent pictures are considered by many people in the west as among the finest images ever from Africa. The book also contains excellent pictures by David Stewart-Smith, a contemporary photographer who first went to the Nuba Mountains in 1995.

Finally I would like to dedicate this book to the many thousands of Nuba who gave their lives fighting for justice, equality, democracy and freedom in Sudan. It is also to be dedicated to the courageous freedom fighters in Southern Kordofan who are still fighting against the odds defending the Nuba land and the right to be Nuba in the Sudan.

Acknowledgements

Much of this book is the outcome of collective efforts by the Nuba and their friends. This book has come out at the right time as the long conflict of the Sudan is taking a new dimension, particularly with recent involvement of countries in the region and internationally, trying to find a peace settlement in the Sudan. It would be unfair if the Nuba political rights, including the rights to self-determination are ignored.

International Nuba Co-ordination Centre (INCC) is greatly indebted to NOVIB and CIIR for taking interest in the book and providing support for its publication. INCC would like to thank David Flower and Julie Flint who took part in the editing.

We are grateful to those who contributed papers to the international Nuba conference of 1996. We are particularly grateful to Mrs. Jinx Rodger for donating some of George Rodger's magnificent photographs to be used in this book. We would also like to thank David-Stewart Smith donating his excellent contemporary photographs on the Nuba.

INCC would like to express its gratitude to Alex de Waal for his useful comments, advice, immense contribution in editing, and his encouragement to go ahead with the production this Nuba book.

London, March 2000

Glossary

DUP	Democratic Unionist Party
GUNM	General Union of the Nuba Mountains
IGAD	Inter-Governmental Authority on Development
INCC	International Nuba Coordination Centre
NGO	Non-Governmental Organisation
NIF	National Islamic Front
NMSA	Nuba Mountains Solidarity Abroad
NRRDO	Nub Relief, Rehabilitation and Development Organisation
PDF	Popular Defence Forces
SNP	Sudan National Party
SPLA	Sudan People's Liberation Army
SPLM	Sudan People's Liberation Movement
UNDP	United Nations Development Programme
UNICEF	United Nations Children's Fund
WFP	World Food Programme of the United Nations

1

The Right to be Nuba

Alex de Waal

Ten years ago, the Nuba of Sudan were politically invisible. Nuba intellectuals and community leaders were being murdered by the Sudan Government with complete impunity. When, in the dark days of 1992, the National Islamic Front planned and launched its *Jihad* and began the massive forced removal of the Nuba people from their ancestral homeland, almost nothing was known about these crimes in the outside world. Even for Sudanese, the war in the Nuba Mountains was hidden: the government said nothing, and the Sudan People's Liberation Army (SPLA) leadership was cut off from its Nuba forces. It seemed, in this darkness, that the Nuba would be consigned to oblivion. They were facing their genocide alone.

The situation is now dramatically and irreversibly changed. Through the efforts of Nuba citizens and leaders, supported by a few outside individuals and organisations, the Nuba are well and truly on the political map. Although the Sudan Government still tries every ruse to deny access to international organisations, and repeatedly boasts that the Nuba rebellion has been "crushed", the world is now well-informed about the struggle of the Nuba people for justice and equality in Sudan. The Nuba issue is on the agenda for peace talks at the Inter-Governmental Authority for Development (IGAD). Nuba leaders are visible in international conferences and the news media. The Nuba Mountains Solidarity Abroad and its newsletter NAFIR have an international reputation. The Nub Relief, Rehabilitation and Development Organisation (NRRDO) have become one of the most widely respected Sudanese humanitarian agencies, receiving support from an ever-widening range of international donors. The amount of aid it can deliver relative to need remains small, but it is providing practical assistance and moral solidarity as the Nuba people face their adversity. Human rights organisations have documented the plight of the Nuba, beginning with African Rights' *Facing Genocide: The Nuba of Sudan* (July 1995), and the most effective on-going human rights monitoring programme in Sudan operating in the Nuba Mountains. Journalists readily travel to the Nuba Mountains, and a series of films about the Nuba has been made and screened by the BBC and other international media-the first and finest being Julie Flint's "The Nuba: Sudan's Secret War," first screened in July 1995.

The Nuba people are still bearing the heavy burden of a vicious war conducted largely against the civilian population. The Sudan Government still uses the weapons of burning villages, removing the people, rape, pillage and murder, as well as inflicting famine and doing its level best to prevent any relief from reaching the people. In any serious practical sense, the international community has not come to the rescue of the Nuba. On 8th of February 2000, an aerial bombardment of Kauda village killed fourteen school children and one teacher. Although only one in a long line of such atrocities (35 school children have been killed in bombing raids since 1997 alone), this one caught the eye the headlines, and briefly the Nuba received the media attention they deserve. In 1999, the United Nations made its first assessment missions to the area, after many years of inaction and delay. But whether there will be effective humanitarian programmes in the area remains to be seen. The political will of the international community to assist the Nuba has proved disappointing.

But now, the international community no longer has the excuse that it does not know. Journalists and human rights workers have all been to the Nuba Mountains, and have witnessed the struggle, the democratic and judicial institutions that function there, and the relentless abuses perpetrated against the people. There are many gestures of solidarity and assistance from individuals and sympathetic non-governmental organisations (NGOs), which are gratefully received. Knowing that there is worldwide recognition for the Nuba cause is an important boost to the morale and determination of the people. But it has not turned the tide. The future of the Nuba people still hangs in the balance. The days when the Sudan Government could contemplate completely eradicating the Nuba, or removing them from the Mountains altogether, are now gone. But the danger still exists that the Nuba political future will be sold away; that a future constitutional settlement in Sudan will leave the Nuba without guarantees for their rights, or as second-class citizens in their own country, with only some nominal "regional autonomy" as a palliative. All Sudanese hope for an end to the current war and the enormous human suffering that it is bringing, but should there be a peace agreement, the Nuba recognise that they may still have a huge political struggle ahead.

The most remarkable aspect of the Nuba struggle today is the spirit of resilience and self-reliance in the people. When I first travelled to the liberated areas of the Nuba Mountains in 1995, with my colleague Yoanes Ajawin to document the human rights situation, the most striking aspect of our experience was not the appalling suffering and poverty of the people, but the amazing spirit of resistance and renewal that existed among these people who had undergone so much. Having been brought right to the brink of annihilation, having, as it were, looked into the abyss of total destruction, and then continued with their struggle, the Nuba people have found a strength and self-confidence that is unsurpassed. The role of outsiders, whether they be human rights activists, aid workers or journalists, is solely to support their struggle.

A key aspect of the Nuba struggle is the fight for the right to "be Nuba". In the liberated Nuba Mountains today there is a cultural renaissance. Traditional dancing, wrestling, music, body painting and a range of other social, cultural and religious practices are being revived and consolidated. Some of these practices are extremely picturesque and, to the western outsider, rather exotic. A number of excellent photographers have recently visited the area and produced stunning pictures of Nuba life and culture, echoing the classic works of George Rodger and Leni Riefenstahl. But these are much more than cultural. For the Nuba, the right to dance is fundamental to their right to exercise their identity. One of the basic reasons for their rebellion was that the Khartoum government was slowly but inexorably undermining these rights. The Nuba were no longer being acknowledged for who they really are; their identity was being crushed.

There was and still exists a programme bent on the eradication and crushing of the Nuba identity, in the name of the 'civilization project' of the Sudan Government. The seizure of farmland, the neglect and closure of schools, the murder of community leaders, the removal of villagers to "peace camps" and other measures are much more concrete and violent manifestations of this policy than attempts to restrict dancing and wrestling. In earlier decades, the process of assimilation to the dominant, Arabised and Islamised Sudanese identity was more peaceable. Nuba learned Arabic, lived in town houses and adopted "Sudanese" culture because it was fashionable, because it was a means of gaining access to salaried employment and education for one's children, and because it enabled Nuba citizens to be part of two worlds at the same time: the national, cosmopolitan culture and the local Nuba culture. But when this process of assimilation became too violent, too racist and too exploitative, the Nuba turned to armed resistance. In that struggle, they have rebuilt their confidence and identity. When peace comes, the Nuba will become citizens of a new peaceful Sudan with an unprecedented sense of their rights as citizens.

One of the great dilemmas that will face Sudan in a future transition to democracy will be the challenge of how to balance liberal rights and the collective rights of the marginalized. This may in fact be the greatest challenge, the issue on which democracy will succeed or fail. Liberals point, with some justification, to the virtues of a unitary state with no restrictions or privileges for any one group. They point to the perils of politicised ethnicity, and how in countries such as Yugoslavia the attempt to brand people with ethnic labels contributed to an extremely bloody war and the break up of the state. They also explain how when collective rights are awarded to an ethnic or religious group, these can be abused to oppress people in the name of customary law and preserving an ethnic identity.

Unfortunately, the Nuba and other marginalised people in Sudan are in no mood to take liberal guarantees at face value. The history of the Nuba Mountains has been that, irrespective of any constitutional or legal guarantees on individual rights, the Nuba have suffered collective oppression, and demand collective guarantees for the future. Their assertion of collective rights, to land, to self-administration, to self-determination, may run in contradiction with certain liberal values, but they see the alternative as continuing marginalisation and even annihilation. The great majority of

Nuba are committed unionists and firmly believe that the Nuba are best served by a united secular Sudanese State with guarantees for all. But should that fail to happen, they reserve their right to consider whatever option is best for their people.

It will not be easy to negotiate a formula that can make this balance work. Individual liberties for all citizens are fundamental, but collective survival for a historically marginalized people who have faced the very real threat of annihilation is just as fundamental. Having shown that they cannot be defeated by war and oppression, the moment will soon come for the Nuba leadership to negotiate their way through these difficult dilemmas.

This book has been produced to educate and enlighten all those who are concerned about the Nuba. It brings together contributions on the history, culture and struggle of the Nuba people, on the abuses they have suffered and their hopes for the future. It is concerned with the identity of the Nuba people, their livelihood, their continuing struggle for rights and justice, and their hopes for the future. Above all, it is an on going effort by the Nuba people to present themselves as they like to be seen to the world.

2

The Nuba

Ahmed Abdel Rahman Saeed

Introduction

The Nuba live in the geographical centre of Sudan, occupying the most fertile agricultural land in the country and have some of its richest and most varied cultures. But they have been reduced to destitution, pushed to the margins of Sudanese politics and society.

After years of onslaught from the Sudan government, including aerial bombing and a murderous "scorched earth" policy, the vitality of the culture of the Nuba people still survives. In the face of organised attempts to destroy them and their culture, the Nuba people's resistance and sense of identity has not diminished, in fact, it has grown stronger.

Who, then, are the Nuba? The term "Nuba" is commonly used to refer to the indigenous inhabitants of the more than eighty small hill communities of the Nuba Mountains of Kordofan Province. A variant of the same name, Nubian, is used to describe the people who lived between Aswan in southern Egypt and the Dongola region of northern Sudan until the High Dam at Aswan was built in 1962-65.[1] In the past, the two names were used interchangeably to describe the people who lived north of Meroe and south of Aswan. Thus, despite the physical and cultural differences between the "Nuba" of the Nuba Mountains (sometimes referred to as Negroid Nubians) and the "Nubians" of the Nile valley (sometimes called Red Nubians), there appears to be a historical connection between the two groups. Exactly what this connection has been the subject of much controversy and no coherent view has emerged to this day. And so, before we introduce the main hypotheses about the early migrations of the Nuba, it may be of some interest to consider the origin of the names Nubian and Nuba.

"Nubia", as applied to the country of the Nubians, seems to have been of western and comparatively modern origin. The word "Nubian" cannot with any certainty be traced further than the Hellenistic[2] and Roman writers. Sir Harold MacMichael[3] quotes the passages in which various forms of Nuba and/or Nubian are referred to as people in the early inscriptions and writings. He mentioned Noba, Nobatae, Noubai, Nubei, Nobae, etc. It was his testimony that Eratosthenes[4] (Ca. 276-194 BC) appears to be the first recorded user of the term, speaking of Noubai north of Meroe and west of the Nile, as far as the "bends of the river." Many possible derivations of the names Nubae, Nubei, Nobatae, etc., have been suggested. MacMichael suggested that the name Nubian is found in the word "nebed" used in an inscription by Thomes I (Ca. 1450 BC) to designate the "curly-haired one", or the "plaited-haired one", who was overthrown by the monarch in the neighbourhood of the third cataract. One other derivation may be from the hieroglyphic word "nb" or "Nubu" meaning "gold", for gold and slaves have been the chief attraction of the Sudan since ancient times.

It is therefore apparent that the present use of the terms Nuba and Nubians as distinct ethnic entities are, in many ways, inaccurate and misleading. Historically the two terms meant the same thing - black - and were used to refer to one racial group. By literal license, Nuba and Nubians came to be synonymous with black or even African,[5] especially from the Northeast of Africa.

The Nuba people and their country

The Nuba are a Negro people encircled by groups of Arabs and Nilotes.[6] They are described as "vigorous hill people of good physique, much independence of mind, strong in tradition and fighting qualities."[7] In 1873, Fr. Stanislao Carcereri, a member of the Camillian Order described them as frank, sincere, cheerful and very intelligent.[8] They live on, or in the vicinity of, hills or jebels known as the Nuba Mountains. The Nuba Mountains region is situated in South Kordofan province, in the very centre of Sudan, between longitude 29 and 31 E and latitude 10 and 12 30 N. It encompasses an area of approximately 30,000 square miles (about 77,700 sq. km), more than four times the size of Kuwait, roughly the size of Scotland. The census of 1983 estimated the population of the Nuba districts to be 1,030,000, nearly 5% of the total population of Sudan.

The Nuba are skilled and energetic cultivators. They possess relatively few cattle and their herds do not have the importance in their lives that they have among the Nilotes. They produce millet, sesame and other crops for their yearly needs.

Although they are distinguished by their height above the surrounding plains, clay lowlands to the south and sandy savannahs to the north, the Nuba Mountains do not form a single, unbroken range but rather consist of clusters of peaks and hill massifs rising, as

Stevenson wrote, "like the islands in an archipelago."[10] The analogy is apt, as Janet Ewald noted.[11] Like an island, each separate peak or massif forms a discrete unit. But like members of an archipelago, each island-hill lies within more or less easy reach of its neighbours. Like the sea, pediplains surround the peaks and massifs and the lowland corridors running through the hill region channel rainwater from the slopes into seasonal watercourses or *khyran*. The hill country itself is well watered. Although intensive cultivation of the hillsides has resulted in considerable deforestation in recent years, they still have a much richer vegetation and thicker woodland than the surrounding plains.

The Nuba display a great amount of diversity and despite certain similarities vary considerably in ethnic stock, culture and language. Because of the nature of the land, their custom of staying to their own hills as much as possible and the dangers of travelling across warring tribes, the Nuba have been isolated even from each other. As a result, each community has tended to develop along its own lines and create its own customs. This is so much the case that the Nuba of the extreme South have, in many ways, as much in common with the Shilluk and Dinka as with the Nuba of the Northern Nuba Mountains.[12] By Nadel's criteria, there are more than 50 ethnic groups in the Nuba Mountains.[13] Greenberg identified 33 languages in the Nuba hills, separating them into Kordofanian and Chari-Nile groups.[14]

Although some researchers have disputed Greenberg's classifications, none doubt the linguistic diversity of the Nuba Mountains. According to James Faris, there are perhaps up to one hundred mutually unintelligible vernaculars in the Nuba hills and some ten distinct groups of languages representing at least two (Niger-Congo and Nilo-Saharan) of Africa's five distinct, unrelated linguistic stocks.[15] The majority of the people also speak Arabic as a lingua franca. The linguistic diversity and complexity of the Nuba peoples, and the similarities with other northern Sudanese languages, have led some researchers to suggest that the Nuba Mountains may historically have been a place of refuge.

In the view of Roland Stevenson, it is "only in reference to the [speakers of hill Nubian] that the name 'Nuba' is historically justified; in the case of the other [groups] it is a misnomer."[16] Stevenson identified ten language groups among the Nuba, each divided into subgroups.[17]

(1) Koalib-Moro
   (a) Koalib
   (b) Heiban, Laro, Otoro
   (c) Shawai, Tira, Moro, Fungor (with Kau and Nyaro)

(2) Talodi-Mesakin
   (a) Talodi
   (b) Eliri
   (c) Mesakin
   (d) Acheron, Tacho, Torona, Kuku-Lumun (a dialect cluster in

Moro hills.)

(3) Lafofa - Lafofa and Amira

(4) Tegali-Tagoi
(a) Tegali sub-group: Tegali, Rashad, Kajakja
(b) Tagoi sub-group: Tagoi, Tumale, Moreib

(5) Kadugli-Korongo
(a) Tullishi, Keiga, Kanga
(b) Miri, Kadugli, Katcha, Tumma,
(c) Korongo, Tumtum

(6) Temein
(a) Temein
(b) Keiga Jirru, Teisei-Umm-Danab

(7) Katla
(a) Katla and Julud
(b) Tima

(8) Nyimang
(a) Nyimang
(b) Affiti (Eastern part of jebel Dair)

(9) Hill Nubian
(a) Dair, Kadaru, Ghulfan and dialect of some small western hills (Tabag, Abu Jinuk)
(b) Dilling, Western Kadaru, Karko, Wali

(10) Daju
(a) Daju of western Kordofan (near Lagawa)
(b) Liguri
(c) Shatt

These linguistic divisions do not coincide with the boundaries of the hill ranges, nor do the linguistic barriers create impermeable social boundaries. Nuba living in the same hill range may speak different languages while others living far apart may share a common language; languages may be different among people who have similar social customs.[18] Dr. Weald has suggested that the most likely reason for this is the historic ebb and flow of the Nuba people. "In response to the natural and human environment, famine and plenty, attacks from the plains or peace, people either scattered across the pediplains or retreated into certain highland regions."[19]

Early Nuba history

It is difficult to date the various Nuba customs because little is known about their history. There is no oral history of the traditions of any hill Nuba community except the Tegali until the twentieth century. And even for the Tegali, primary written sources begin to corroborate oral evidence only in the nineteenth century.[20] However, we will present a number of historical arguments in order to attempt as reliable a construction as is possible of Nuba history.

Certain Nuba, for example Dilling, Dair, Kadaru, Ghulfan, Karko, speak languages with clear Nubian affinities. This has led some historians to make a racial connection between the Nuba of Southern Kordofan and the Nilotic

Nubians. Others dispute this theory in view of the utter dissimilarity of the two groups both physically and culturally and suggest that the language of the Negroid Nuba acquired its Nubian features as a result of the relatively recent Dongolawi immigration to Kordofan. Professor Zyhlarz[21] has shown that "Hill Nubian" and "Nilotic Nubian" are separate branches of the Nuba language, each characterised by distinctive features of its own. It follows that the assumption of one group "borrowing" its language from the other can no longer be upheld.

Zyhlarz propounds a theory of Nubian (or Nuba for that matter) migration according to which Kordofan, and not the Nile Valley, is the homeland of Nubian speech and of the Nubian race. According to this theory, the dispersion of the people, and therefore the language, occurred at a much earlier date than was previously thought.

MacMichael, like Seligman,[22] rejects the suggestion of a racial connection between the Hill Nuba and the Nilotic Nuba and attributes the linguistic affinities of the two groups to the immigration of the Nilotic colonists to Southern Kordofan. He claims that after the Arabs overthrew the Christian Kingdom of Dongola and established themselves in the area, they rapidly amalgamated with the local Nubians and sent the Barabra (who speak a language unlike that of the northern Nuba of Southern Kordofan) into Kordofan, where they settled around the most northerly of the Nuba Mountains. These immigrants intermarried with the Negroes, who were probably descendants of the erstwhile conquerors of Nubia, and imposed their own language upon them.

Hillelson[23] refutes the above claims and concludes that "it was the Nobatae or Nuba who, in classical times, brought the Nubian language from Kordofan to the Nile valley and they imposed it upon the people of different race in whom they became absorbed." He bases his conclusion not only on the dialectical differences between the Nilotic and Hill Nubian (in itself a very strong point) but also on other considerations.

Firstly, if the Barabra colonists so profoundly influenced the Hill Nuba in the matter of language, as claimed by MacMichael and Seligman, this contact should have left some mark on their customs and their culture. Yet there is no trace of cultural influence, a fact that led Seligman to reject any racial connection between the two groups.

Secondly, although there are strong grounds for connecting the Nubian language with the Sudanic group of languages of upper Nile that include Dinka and Bari, it cannot in any sense be classified as a Hamitic language.

Last but not least, although the inhabitants of the lower Nile Valley have been called "Nubian" since the dawn of history, there is no evidence that the people who dwelt there either spoke Nubian or were called by that name at any date before that fixed by Zyhlarz for the arrival of the migrants of Kordofan.

To conclude, let us quote Hillelson:[24] "The use of the term Nubian as designating any part of the Nile Valley or its population previous to the Hellenistic age is unjustified. The true classical names are Ethiopia and Meroe. The true Nubians were a Negroid people of Kordofan, offshoots of which settled in the Nile Valley and at Gebel Midob. The mixed people of the Nile Valley (Meroitic Ethiopians, etc.), in which these settlers are absorbed, adopted the Nubian language and the Nubian name. These are the Christian Nubians of the Middle Ages. After the Arab invasions, the Christian Nubians adopted Islam and received a large admixture of Arab blood."

Furthermore, the word Kordofan, which took its name from a mountain a few miles south-east of El-Obeid, is itself believed to be of Nuba origin.[25] The meaning of the first syllable, "Kordu", is "man" and the other syllable, "fan", means "country". Therefore, "Kordufan" may mean "the land of men", i.e. "the inhabited country" or "the cultivable country".

Nuba Custom and Traditions

Despite the apparent racial, ethnic and linguistic diversity of the Nuba, there is a cultural tendency which can be called a "Nuba culture" common to all the various groups. It may not pervade the whole of cultural life, but it goes deeper than a common way of life or a cultural affinity that could be explained as an adjustment of dissimilar groups to identical conditions of life.[26] Nonetheless, in spite of this common "Nuba culture", there exists, on a smaller scale, other features of cultural individuality which distinguish each single tribe, or tribal section, from the other. We will therefore try to concentrate on customs and traditions common to all Nuba tribes and here it is interesting to note that Nuba customs arise almost entirely out of religion.

Kujurism: The Traditional Religion of the Nuba.

The Nuba revere and honour their ancestors. This tradition is so prevalent that it seems to overshadow the concept of deity. The veneration of Ancestral Spirit in Nuba tradition, a veneration that comes close to worship, forms the basis of Nuba religion. It also explains the Nuba's exceptional tribal patriotism, their reluctance to leave their ancestors' home, their reverence for the dead and tribal elders, their fervid desire for children, and so forth.

"Curse a Nuba and he may forgive you," says Hawkesworth. "Curse his ancestor and you become his enemy for ever."[27] Each Nuba tribe sees in its ancestor the tribal "god" who directs his descendants' fate and sends all blessings and all calamities including death, a punishment for transgressing the ordinance of ancestral tradition. Communications are addressed not to God but to the Ancestral Spirit. Usually supported by gifts, they are made through a medium or tribal priest called by different names in different tribes but popularly known as a Kujur.[28] Kujurs act as the Ancestral Spirits' mouthpieces and are believed to be possessed by them on certain occasions. Herein lies the fundamental difference between the concept of Kujurism in the Nuba tradition and the magicians, witch doctors and rain-makers of other African tribes: the Kujur seeks to propitiate the powers that be; magicians and witch-doctors seek to control them. Kujurs act as servants of the god or gods they worship; magicians act as masters and aim to control both natural and supernatural agencies.

Kujurs are first and foremost mediators between the people and their Ancestral Spirit. They use their powers to induce the Ancestral Spirit to hand down blessings and punishments. If they do not receive the customary offerings of grain before rains, they use their influence to invoke evil. The rewards for good deeds are happiness, abundant crops, fertility, victory in war and long life. Punishment means bad rain, plagues of locust, sterility, plagues on men and cattle, defeat in war and death.

In addition to the spirit of the original ancestor, there are numerous lesser spirits belonging to different family groups. It is believed that these spirits may act together in council, the greater spirit acting as chief over them. The lesser spirits are generally experts in one particular branch of culture. One may be an expert on rain, another on crops or cattle, a third on trees, goats, war etc. If any of the lesser Kujurs is negligent in his duties, the Great Kujur gathers together the elders of the tribe and demands an explanation for this neglect. Among most Nuba tribes, the Great Kujurs represent the patriarchal heads of the tribes, exercising both spiritual and secular powers. Exceptions to this are to be found among the Dilling, Afitti, Nyimang, Kadero and Kalero groups, where the office of King exists in addition to that of the Kujur. However, the Great Kujur is always the supreme head, even above the King. There is evidence to suggest that Kingship is a comparatively recent institution derived from the Nuba who acted as intermediaries when the Nuba came into contact with the Arab tribes of the North.

Kujurs are regarded as sacred. They eat alone and in privacy. Only a fellow Kujur or a father of twins[29] may share their seats. Anyone greeting the Kujur should bare his left shoulder to receive a blessing. Although the office of Kujur is not hereditary and the Ancestral Spirit can seize upon any person in the clan, it often happens, especially among the lesser Kujurs, that the Spirit selects the offspring of the deceased Kujur. Furthermore, the office of Kujur is not confined to the male sex. The Great Kujuria of Kunit, Hamra Bitt Gamal, who died in 1926, was one of the most revered and feared rainmakers in the region[30], although a female Kujur must be a married woman with children and must be a descendent of the deceased Kujur. It sometimes happens that the spirit forsakes one Kujur and seizes upon another.

Every Kujur has a special house in his enclosure known as the house of the Ancestral Spirit and where spears and other appurtenances of office are kept. In most hills, these houses are distinguished by ostrich eggs covered with splotches of paints and set on the apex of the hut. The Kujurs themselves wear a number of metal bracelets and rings as the symbol of their office and carry some sort of stick or axe adorned with brass wire or some other kind of metal. When a Kujur dies, he enjoys the honour of being buried in his house. All his offspring, male and female, married and unmarried, must remain celibate for a period of one or two years. It is believed that failure to observe this custom may result in the death of the guilty person.

In summary, the Nuba religion plays a vital role in the social life of Nuba communities. Their reverence for the supernatural powers of their Ancestral Spirits, and their sacred shrines, provides the strength of their culture and traditions and their respect for private property, the sanctity of marriage and human life. Should anyone undermine these religious beliefs, the whole social structure will collapse. The Nuba religion has survived the strain of more than one invasion in the past. Today a more powerful enemy threatens its survival, disguised in the mantles of Islamisation and Arabisation.

Status of Women in the Nuba Community

In contrast with many other communities in the Sudan, the Nuba woman is "a happy one" and her influence in society cannot be overlooked. She is not barred from any religious or social functions and may enter the Kujur's hut and other holy places just as men. Many become powerful Kujuria, the Great Kujuria of Kunit being an outstanding example. One of the powerful ginadi[31] of Dilling must be a woman, to represent her sex in affairs of state and in judicial matters.

The influence of women, however, varies from tribe to tribe. In Kunit, special dances are held during the harvest festival (which lasts for two to three months) in which only women and Kujurs are allowed to participate.

Women eat apart from men, and are responsible for household duties such as cooking, fetching of water and collecting firewood. They are expected to help in cultivation although strenuous work like the building of houses and the clearing of ground for cultivation is reserved for men. Faris noted that "in most [Nuba] communities, especially in those not yet converted to Islam, women have considerable freedom and often farm on their own land. Indeed, they are probably among the freest women in Sudan."[32]

Although there are some cases where young girls have been married against their wishes, the girl's wishes are often taken into account. Clitoridectomy is regarded as an initiation ritual and the final marriage ceremony cannot take place until the operation has been performed. There are a few exceptions, the Nyimang tribe for example, where no form of female circumcision is practised. Recently, the Sudan People's Liberation Movement has outlawed the practice in the areas that it controls, and this prohibition is reported to be well enforced.

It is a moot point whether this custom originates from or pre-dates contact with the Arabs. Clitoridectomy among the Nuba differs from the Pharaonic and Sunna forms of the Arabs. It involves the cutting of the clitoris only, not the labia, and does not involve stitches. The operation is performed at different times by different tribes. In Wali, Kunit and Fanda, the operation takes place before a girl loses her virginity. Among the Dilling, Kaderu, Ghulfan and Kudur, it is performed during the last period of pregnancy. In Mandal, it coincides with the approach or onset of puberty.

Betrothal and Marriage

Most Nuba youths begin courting at about the age of twenty. He generally becomes engaged when the girl is still a child although sexual intercourse is permitted only when the girl reaches puberty. Marriage rules may differ slightly from one hill to another, but the general principles are essentially the same. As a general rule, there are two parts to marriage: the betrothal ceremony, and the final marriage ceremony. The first period, which usually lasts for several years, is regarded as essentially pre-marital. Relations may be broken by either party, without detriment, if they prove unsatisfactory. Sometimes, as in the Fanda hills, spiritual assistance is employed to decide marriage.

When wishing to marry, the man approaches the girl first. If she approves, she will encourage him to approach her parents and make enquiries as to the number of cattle and/or goats required as "bride price". The number of cattle paid as dowry[33] varies, but, until war enveloped the mountains in the 1980s, averaged about eight. The man usually sends two old women to approach the girl's parents. If they consent, the village will be informed of the engagement. The man then visits the girl at night, accompanied by a male friend of his own age and carrying gifts. The girl invites a female friend. These two friends are witnesses to the occasion. The women anoint the arms of the men, and although deflowering is not permitted during this first night, the man is allowed to sleep with his fiancee.

After the betrothal ceremony, the pair live as man and wife to all intents and purposes although the woman cannot proceed to the man's house and take up her household duties there. The man builds a small hut in the precincts of his in-law's house. He may not live there, but he is allowed to visit and spend the night with his betrothed whenever he wishes. Moreover, it is incumbent on the would-be bridegroom to work for his future in-laws in their cultivation. It is of paramount importance that the suitor wins the approval of the girl's parents, for it is only with their consent that the marriage can take place. The more he works the more he is appreciated. This rendering of service, which must continue each year until the final marriage ceremony, is cited by Hawkesworth as evidence of the wisdom of the Nuba and the perfection of their customs.[34] For it provides against the unscrupulous man who prefers to flit from flower to flower instead of binding himself with the bond of marriage and deters the would-be husband from delaying the final ceremony too long.

There is no limit to the time of payment of the bride price. On payment of part of the bride price, the bridegroom is permitted to begin conjugal relations with his bride who, however, continues to live in her parents' house until she bears a child. The husband then completes half of the payment for his wife and takes her to his own house. The remaining half is usually paid either when the offspring of the marriage grow up or from the marriage payments made for the daughters. If there are no daughters, the sons are responsible for completing the contract. If the husband dies before the payment is made good, his heirs must pay off the remainder of the debt.

The final marriage ceremony takes place when the bride enters the home of the bridegroom. The bridal pair enter the house together, led by the best man. The bridegroom sends some food to the house of the Kujur, and the bride spends her first night in the house of her betrothed. The weeks following are spent in feasting, drinking and dancing. During this period, the bride may not cook or partake in the eating or preparing of the food of the house. However, on the last day of this ceremony, she cooks her favourite dish, which is solemnly tasted by all present, and the rest of the day is spent in dancing and feasting. The marriage has at last been consummated and the bridal pair have been joined together till death parts them, it being ordained by custom that divorce is impossible after this ceremony.

Sagar[35], in his notes on the Nuba customs, says that the right of divorce is recognised by some Nuba tribes, including the Dilling, even though it is extended in some cases only to men. Hawkesworth believes that Sagar is probably confusing the betrothal period with the marriage proper.[36] What is certain, however, is that in recent years certain tribes have deviated from custom although all agree that traditional law excludes divorce and no true Nuba would dare to contravene it.

Polygamy is practised in most Nuba tribes. A Nuba may in theory marry as many wives as he can afford to keep, although in practice many men have just one wife, or two at the most. Each wife has her own household and the husband's attention to them is regulated by custom. It is interesting to note that, in some tribes, a man may not marry the daughter of his father's brother although he may marry the daughter of his father's sister, or any cousin on his mother's side. Sagar interprets this an as indication that some Nuba tribes consider relationship through the male line stronger than through the female.

Sowing and Harvesting Festivals

The religious and social aspects of agriculture play a very important part in Nuba life. Although farming methods and the forms of belief connected with them may differ in detail from one hill to another, the underlying features are essentially the same. The time for sowing and harvesting is closely regulated and controlled, not by the individual farmers, but by the Kujur.

There are two main festivals in the Nuba year: one when crops are sown, and another when they ripen. The Kujur's plot is generally the first to be sown and often ceremonially so, with each farmer assisting. When the rain begins to fall, each Nuba takes a measure of the previous year's grain to the Kujur and, on a given day, all assemble. The Kujur chooses a small patch of ground and surrounds it with a fence. He then sows a few handfuls of the grain and sprinkles over it the blood of a lamb, the blood of a cock and some marissa (local beer made from fermented grain) from last year's grain. After this, all the congregation feast and dance for several days. Then they wait until the planted shoots show about a hand's breadth above the ground.

If the seed grows well and plentifully, it is taken as a sign that the harvest will be good and all the people sow as much as possible. If, on the other hand, the Kujur's seed grows badly, it is said that the harvest will be poor and a minimum of grain is sown.

At the beginning of the harvest, each Nuba takes a few heads of his dura to the Kujur, who, after consultation with his Ancestral Spirit, announces that the crops are fit for harvesting. This festival is regarded as a harvest thanks-giving ceremony. Far more elaborate rites surround the harvest, and particularly the harvest of the first fruits, than any other stage of Nuba agriculture. The first crops to ripen are najjad (an early-maturing variety of dura), maize (Indian/sweet corn) and lubia (peas or beans). The first-fruit ceremonies usually embrace all three and are characterised by drinking of marissa and ceremonial gathering of the first of the early crops, the cutting of which is prohibited until the ceremony has taken place.

Another important festival is for the fertility of animals. Before the cattle-breeding season commences, all the children of a village turn out to collect ants' eggs. They are given to the Kujur, who throws them over the cattle of the village as they are driven past. It is, however, considered unlucky for a cow to give birth to two calves at a time. Whenever this happens, the cow and her calves are turned out of the herd and disposed of at the earliest opportunity by gift, sale or exchange.

Impact of Islam in the Nuba Mountains

The Nuba were exposed to the influence of Islam as far back as the early sixteenth century. Before that time, the Nuba inhabited the whole of Kordofan. But after the collapse of the Christian kingdoms, Islam triumphed in the Nile valley and Muslim groups claiming Arab ancestry began a southward migration which took them to central Kordofan where they settled and intermarried with some of the indigenous Nuba population.[37] Two processes resulted from this immigration, settlement and intermarriage. On one hand, some of the Nuba were Islamised and acquired Arabic language and culture. On the other, Islam itself was indigenised and the Arabs were absorbed to varying degrees.[38]

Under pressure from the Muslim Arabs' invasion and in order to avoid cultural absorption and slave raiding, the Nuba retreated to their present homeland in the Nuba Mountains. Those who made the journey southward were able to take refuge in the hills and hence maintained their cultural identity and independence. However, small groups of Nuba remained in the outlying hills of Kordofan—Haraza, Katul, Abu Hadid, Kaja, etc.—and are now largely Islamized and Arabised.

The extent of the spread of Islam among the Nuba varies considerably from one hill community to another, with Nuba chiefs contributing to a large extent both to the spread of Islam and its uneven distribution. Many Nuba chiefs professed an allegiance to Islam for reasons of personal ambition, to attain a "higher" social status by belonging to the religion of the "aristocratic" group. In compact, more centralized communities such as Tegali, Dilling and Tira, the community leaders (Mukuk, Kings, or chiefs) accepted Islam not as a religion per se but rather as a symbol of aristocracy, in order to enhance their own superiority. They used their authority to impose it on their people and make some superficial changes in tribal customs. In contrast, in subdivided, widely scattered communities such as in Kawalib, Nyimang and Moro, there was no one individual leader to impose a regime upon others so that these communities were less receptive to Islamic influence.[39]

Tegali is the closest part of the Nuba Mountains to the centres of Arab migration and Islamic culture in northern Sudan. It has been considered as the "cradle of Islam" in the Nuba Mountains[40] because it was the first area in the Nuba Mountains to be influenced by Islam. This influence initially came about initially not through Arab/Muslim immigration, but through the agency of a single Muslim "Arab Stranger" known as Mohammed al-Ja'ali who settled in Tegali around 1530.[41]

Slave raiding had threatened the Nuba Mountains ever since Muslim Arabs came into contact with the Nuba in the early sixteenth Century. In the violent context of slave raiding and trading, Islam assumed a special meaning in Tegali. In theory, Islamic law prohibits Muslims from seizing other Muslims as slaves, but permits slave raiding against non-Muslims. Therefore, Tegali Mukuk (Kings), more than any other leaders in the Nuba Mountains, adhered to Islam to create a sanctuary from slave raiding. In their quest to protect their communities as well as to justify their own raids, the Tegali Mukuk presented themselves to the outside world first as Muslims then as Arabs.[42] The Tegali Mukuk acted as both protectors and predators.

It has recently been asserted that the Nuba Kingdom of Tegali was an Islamic Kingdom. Such an assertion is misleading and a gross misrepresentation of the historical truth for Islam has never been a political actor in the Tegali Kingdom. While Muslim Kings indeed ruled Tegali and welcomed Muslim clergymen from the Nile valley in their Kingdom, their subjects were allowed complete freedom "to practice their local religions and follow leaders characteristic of the Nuba Mountains."[43] Tegali people, both subjects and Mukuk, resisted the implementation of Islamic (shari'a) law over their lives and were content with their secular, customary law.

Furthermore, the Mahdiya (1885-98) failed to gain any significant support in Tegali despite the Islamic nature of its agenda. This could be attributed, at least in part, to the fact that Islam was not a political issue in Tegali. At best, the Mahdiya regarded Tegali as practising mixed or incomplete Islam. At worst, as bluntly expressed by the Mahdi's Khalifa, "the Tegali people had no faith in God but instead trusted to their weapons."[44]

Although Tegali was exposed to Islam as early as the sixteenth century, Islam did not influence other parts of the Nuba Mountains until the nineteenth century during the Turco-Egyptian rule (1821-1885)—primarily towards its end when slave raiding had receded. During the Mahdiya, some Nuba communities were forced to profess Islam. For example, a large population from Ghulfan, Derbi and Kadero was taken to Omdurman and returned as Muslims.[45] But many Nuba who had been forcibly Islamized reverted when the Mahdist forces were weakened.[46]

Slave raiding and political upheaval during the Turkiya and Mahdiya had two opposing effects regarding the spread of Islam in the Nuba Mountains. On the one hand, they strengthened group solidarity and resistance so that some communities, like the Nyimang, became more resistant to outside influences. On the other hand, the tribal institutions of some smaller communities were undermined so that a few groups were absorbed.

After independence, successive Sudan governments began prosecuting a pro-Islamic policy in the Sudan, disowning any African component in the Sudanese identity and seeing Islam and Arabism as the only basis for integration. In the Nuba Mountains, the Sudanese Ministry of Religious Affairs introduced an intensive Islamisation programme in which Nuba students were chosen from intermediate or secondary schools for

Islamic training and then posted back among their people.[47] Both the African Islamic centre of Khartoum and al-Azhar University in Cairo, Egypt, offer special grants for Nuba Muslims to assist in the spread of Islam in the Nuba Mountains. This "official" policy was, and is, coupled with financial backing from popular Islamic organisations originating in the Gulf. Many mosques were built and Islam and the Arabic language were, and are, taught in all schools in the Nuba Mountains. On many occasions pupils were forced to change their Nuba names to Arabic/Islamic names in a wilful attempt to destroy their heritage and African identity.

Today, the large number of mosques in the urban centres of the Nuba Mountains immediately catches the attention of visitors, giving the impression that the whole Nuba population is Islamized.[48] Most of these mosques are empty, however, and the few that are not are frequented mainly by Baggara and Jellaba.

The main feature of Islam in the Nuba Mountains is that its acceptance causes little disruption to the customs and traditions of Nuba society. Islam has not penetrated the defensive mechanism of Nuba culture but has rather adapted itself to the social life of the Nuba: Nuba Moslems drink marissa and eat pork, and there is seldom any conflict with those who profess traditional beliefs. As a result, Sudan's Arab rulers do not regard Nuba Muslims as proper Muslims.

It can therefore be said that the changes that have taken place as a result of Islam (and perhaps Christianity) have not affected the social fabric of the Nuba. Almost all Nuba Muslims (and Christians) regard themselves as full members of their ethnic groups.[49] Their religious identity (whether Islamic or Christian) takes second place to their ethnic identity.

---

1. The building of the High Dam necessitated massive resettlement of the inhabitants of these villages.
2. Hellenistic period is the period in Greek civilization from the death of Alexander (323 BC) until the accession of the Roman emperor Augustus (27 BC).
3. MacMichael, H. A. "A History of the Arabs in the Sudan", Vol. I, 1922, p. 12.
4. Eratosthenes, Greek geographer and Mathematician, whose map of the ancient world was the first to contain lines of latitude and longitude.
5. Faris, J. C.; "Nuba" in: R. V. Weekes (Editor), Muslim Peoples: A World Ethnographic Survey, 2nd Edition, 1984, pp. 554-559.
6. Nadel, S. F. "The Nuba: An Anthropological Study of the Hill Tribes in Kordofan," Oxford University Press, 1947, p. 1.
7. Stevenson, R. C. "The Nuba people of Kordofan Province: An Ethnographic Survey," Graduate college Publications, Monograph 7, University of Khartoum, 1984, p. 6.
8. Toniolo, E. and R. Hill (eds.), "The opening of the Nile Basin", 1974, p.290.
9. Weekes, R. V. (editor), "Muslim peoples: A World Ethnographic Survey," Aldwych Press, London, England, 1984, p. 922.
10. Stevenson, R. C., *op cit* 1984, p. 6.
11. Ewald, J. J., "Soldiers, Traders, and Slaves: State Formation and Economic Transformation in the Greater Nile Valley, 1700-1885," The University of Wisconsin Press, 1990, p. 21.
12. Sagar, J. W. "Notes on the History, Religion and Customs of the Nuba," Sudan Notes & Records, Vol. V, December 1922, p. 137.
13. Nadel, S. F., *op cit*, pp. 9-10.
14. Greenberg, Joseph, "The languages of Africa," 3rd. Edition, Bloomington, 1970, pp. 163-71.
15. Faris, J., "Muslim Peoples: A World Ethnographic Survey," Weekes, R. (Editor), 1984, p. 555.
16. Hillelson, S. "Nubian Origin," Sudan Notes and Records, Vol. XIII, Part I, 1930, p. 144.

17. Stevenson, R. C., *op cit* , pp 8-9.
18. Stevenson, R. C., *op cit*, p. 7.
19. Ewald, J. J, *op cit.,* p. 24.
20. Ewald, J. J. *op cit.,* p. 19.
21. E. Zyhlarz, "Zur Stellung Darfur-Nubischen," Vienna, 1928, Reviewed by: S. Hillelson, 'Origin of Nubians', Sudan Notes & Records, Vol. XIII, Part I, 1930. pp. 137-148.
22. Seligman, C. G., "Some Aspects of the Hamitic Problem in the Anglo-Egyptian Sudan," J.R.A.I., Vol. XLIII
23. Hillelson, S., "Nubian Origin," A Review of Zyhlarz, Zur Stellung des Darfur-Nubischen, Sudan Notes and Records, Vol. XIII, Part I, 1930, pp. 137-148.
24. Hillelson, S. *op cit..,* p. 144.
25. See MacMichael, H. A. "The Tribes of Northern and Central Kordofan", 1912, pp. 222-224.
26. Nadel, S. F. *op cit..,* pp 3-4.
27. D. Hawkesworth, "The Nuba proper of Southern Kordofan", Sudan Notes and Records, Vol. XV, Part II, 1932, p. 161.
28. It seems that the term kujur originated from the Dilling and their tribal relations (in Wali, Ghulfan, Kaderu, and other hills). The Nyimang call him kuni, the Tima kamal, the Miri tamsala, and the Koalib bayel or bel (see S. F. Nadel, "A Shaman Cult in the Nuba Mountains," Sudan Notes and Records, Vol. XXIV, 1941, p. 85.
29. The parents of twins among the Nuba proper enjoy the same status of Kujurs and are treated with similar respect and reverence. The twins themselves, however, are regarded as normal human beings.
30. Hawkesworth, D., "The Nuba proper of Southern Kordofan", Sudan Notes and Records, Vol. XV, Part II, 1932, p 171.
31. Ginadi (Arabic, sing. gindi) is a system of native administration which existed mainly in the Dilling, Kudur and Mandal hills where each clan of the specific tribe is represented by one person (gindi). The Great Kujur usually delegates part of his powers to this 'ginadi council' to settle disputes and undertake other judicial powers. Their power may sometimes extend to punishing the Great Kujur himself if his work is seen unsatisfactory, e.g. if the rain fails to fall. In the Dilling dialect, this is called Kejat (pl. Keni). One clan of Dilling, known as Sha'mun, is always represented by a woman, who must be a widow (timneri).
32. Faris, James C., "Nuba", in: Muslim Peoples: A World Ethnographic Survey, Richard V. Weekes (Editor), 2nd. Edition, 1984, p. 558.
33. The term 'brideprice' is used for lack of a more appropriate word. There is no idea of buying and selling in the transaction. The woman belongs to the husband not after the bride price has been paid, but after the final marriage ceremony has been performed. The brideprice is rather in the nature of an insurance for the stability of the marriage and a compensation to the woman's group for the loss of a member.
34. Hawkesworth, D.; Sudan Notes and Records, Vol. XV, Part II, 1932, p. 176-177.
35. Sagar, J. W.; "Notes on the History, Religion, and Customs of the Nuba", Sudan Notes and Records, Vol. v, December 1922, PP 137-156.
36. Hawkesworth, D.; *op cit*, p. 184.
37. Trimingham, J. S., Islam in the Sudan, p. 244; also see MacMichael, H. A., The Arabs in the Sudan, Vol. I, 1922, p.34
38. Stevenson, R. C., Some Aspects of the Spread of Islam In the Nuba Mountains, SNR, Vol. 44, 1963, p.9
39. Stevenson, R.C. *op cit*, pp. 9-20,
40. Ibrahim, A. U. M.; "The Dilemma of the British Rule in the Nuba Mountains, 1898-1947", 1985, p.9.
41. Elles, R. J., "The Kingdom of Tegali", *SNR*, Vol. 35, 1935, pp. 1-35.
42. Ewald, J. J., *op cit..,* pp. 137-138.
43. Ewald, J. J. *op.cit.,* p. 15
44. Ewald, J. J. ;*op. cit.,* p. 124.
45. Trimingham, J. S.; "Islam in the Sudan"; second edition, 1965, p.245.
46. Trimingham, J, S., *op. cit.*; p.104.
47. Mohammed-Salih, M. A. R.; "Africanism and Islamism in the Nuba Mountains"; in: S. H. Hurreiz and E. A. Abdel-Salam (eds.), Ethnicity, Conflict and National Integration, Institute of African and Asian Studies, Khartoum, 1989, pp.216-218.
48. Mohammed-Salih, M. A. R.; op. cit., pp.218-219.
49. Manger, L. O.; "From the Mountains to the Plains", 1994, p. 155.

3

The Nuba of South Kordofan

George Rodger

An extract from the diary of George Rodger, written in 1949.

We camped our first night in Kordofan on the southern boundary of the province. It was a hot night and still, and a moon, two-thirds full, gave sufficient light so we could pitch camp without the aid of lanterns. An Arab brought us water that was saline and muddy but quite drinkable and we had supper under the stars and slept with the distance cries of hyenas and the rumbling of lions around us.

The following day we reached the Jebel Country and the road twisted between mountains that were constructed by nature of piled boulders. Stunted poison trees with their wax-like pinkish flowers grew on the stony ground and, in the valleys, were the green, shady haraz trees with their curled yellow seed pods on which the Arabs feed their camels. For the first time we saw the villages of the Nubas. They hung so high and were so much a part of the terrain that it seemed the little pot-bellied huts, with their thatched roofs, had been taken by the handful and hurled against the mountainside to settle in the crevices between the rocks where the wind and the weather and the passage of time had merged them into one with jebels themselves. Some had lodged in sheer-sided ravines, others clung precariously to the bare rock and some were perched jointly on the tops of bald boulders like the fanciful creations of some whimsical milliner. Children ran up and down steep rocky paths as agile as the jebel goats and, at the foot of the jebel, on the flat land, the girls of the village watered their tobacco crops from the large yellow gourds which they carried on their heads from the wells.

At the village called Reika, the Mek of the Masakin Qsar visited us, bringing a live sheep as a present, and told us that a sibr was soon to be held in the neighbouring Korongo jebels. A sibr is a gathering of the people to commemorate a tribal event and, among the Nubas, almost always include a display of their athletic powers. The Korongos, probably on account of their terrific physique, are the finest wrestlers of all the Nuba tribes, so it was an opportunity for us to witness some of the tribal sports we had come so far to see. The sibr began in the middle of the morning under the fierce heat of a sun already high, and the scene was set beneath the heglig trees, below the village of Buram.

When we arrived the wrestlers were seated in the shade of thorn trees talking amongst themselves. They were men of tremendous physique, each one standing well over six feet in height and broad in proportion. They were completely naked and had rubbed their bodies with the white wood-ash so they could get a grip more easily while wrestling. Their heads were shaved except for a few small tufts of hair, which were left for decoration.

A strange procession wound its way down from the village in the jebel preceded by a naked tribesman beating a large drum. Behind him came several women each with a wide shallow bowl balanced on her head. In the bowls there were plumed belts made from the coats of the colobus monkey, ostrich feathers and ornamental armbands. These were to be worn by the fighting men. Behind them came more wrestlers, white with wood-ash, and the rest of the village followed, dancing, singing and waving their spears. All of them, men, women and children, were naked though some had devised special ornaments for the occasion. One girl was decorated with bands made from the metal tops of beer bottles which she wore on strings around her neck and waist. An immense muscular gentleman had a whole heron with widespread wings attached to his back. Another had a band of brass bells strapped around his stomach. Many wore ostrich plums and some who were already covered in wood-ash beautified themselves still further by tracing designs in it with soot. Some of the girls had poured curdled milk over their heads and shoulders so they looked like frosted chocolate cakes but had an odour of their own. The older women had rubbed themselves in sim-sim oil so they were sleek and shiny. At the tail of the procession came fifty young girls carrying gourds of marissa, the native beer, balanced on their head. Their posture was superb and they even danced to the beat of the drum without spilling a drop of the potent drink they were carrying.

As the procession came nearer, the wrestlers detached themselves and advanced, squatting in a crouched position, and flexing their muscle. They grunted in unison with each step and the young girls ran beside them making high pitched trilling sound by passing their tongues rapidly between their lips. Then, without much order the wrestling bouts began. The onlookers formed a rough circle around the competitors who faced each other in pairs. There were half a dozen bouts in progress at the same time. First they crouched and suddenly, without warning, they grappled. The crowd roared encouragement, waved their spears and pressed close for a better view. A medicine man beat the ground with a leather flail to keep away the evil spirits. A dull roar from a thousand throats announced that someone had been thrown and the winner was hosted onto the shoulders of a husky giant to be carried through the throng with the women thrilling in high key before him. It was a stirring scene. Fresh fighters arrived. The women sprinkled them with white ash which they shook from long-necked gourds. The girls passed beer around and another bout began.

We left them in the late evening to return to camp. When the festivals were over we thanked the Mek for his kindness but were not permitted to leave until we had accepted gifts of a chicken, fourteen eggs, two fighting sticks and a shield. The generosity of these people of the jebels to complete strangers was almost overwhelming, and when we left, we took with us memories of a people, primitive it is true, but so much more hospitable and gracious than many of us who live in the dark continents outside Africa.

Photographs on following pages:

Photographs 1-8: With kind permission of the estate of George Rodger. The photographs were taken in 1949.

1. A Sibr gathering: wrestlers spar with each other before the bouts take place.
2. Wrestlers facing each other, Korongo.
3. Korongo wrestling match
4. The victor is carried in triumph on the shoulders of his 'second'.
5. A Korongo girl with cicatrice marking carries a gourd of beer.
6. Nuba girls watering tobacco plants, Mesakin Gisar.
7. Bedroom of Korongo Nuba house. The sole access is through the small hole.
8. In the granary of a Korongo house, two women grind dura to make bread.

Photographs 9-13: Taken by Suleiman Musa Rahhal, 1997.

9. Nuba stick fighters in action, Gidail Sibr.
10. Wrestlers before the bout, Gidail Sibr.
11. Stilt dancers.
12. Kambala dancers, from Kadugli.

13. Nuba Kujur (traditional healer) *Nanne op't Ende, 1999*

14. Suleiman Musa Rahhal

Photographs 15-17 taken by Julie Flint, 1995.

15. Guarding the mountains—Nuba SPLA soldiers.
16. New recruits at SPLA training camp.
17. Yousif Kuwa Mekki receives a blessing from a Kujur (traditional healer).
18. Yousif Kuwa speaks.

A.1. A Sibr gathering: wrestlers spar with each other before the bouts take place.
(*George Rodger, 1949*)

A.2. Wrestlers facing each other, Korongo. (*George Rodger, 1949*)

A.3. Korongo wrestling match
(*George Rodger, 1949*)

A.4. The victor is carried in triumph on the shoulders of his 'second'.
(*George Rodger, 1949*)

A.5. A Korongo girl with cicatrice marking carries a gourd of beer.
(*George Rodger, 1949*)

A.6. Nuba girls watering tobacco plants, Mesakin Gisar.
(*George Rodger, 1949*)

A.7. Bedroom of Korongo Nuba house. The sole access is through the small hole.
(*George Rodger, 1949*)

A.8. In the granary of a Korongo house, two women grind dura to make bread. (*George Rodger, 1949*)

A.9. Nuba stick fighters in action, Gidail, Sibr.
(*Suleiman Musa Rahhal, 1997*)

A.10. Wrestlers before the bout, Gidail Sibr.
(*Suleiman Musa Rahhal, 1997*)

A.12. Kambala dancers, from Kadugli.
(*Suleiman Musa Rahhal, 1997*)

A.11. Stilt dancers.
(*Suleiman Musa Rahhal, 1997*)

A.13. Nuba Kujur (traditional healer), Nanne op't Ende, 1999 (*Suleiman Musa Rahhal, 1997*)

A.14. Suleiman Musa Rahhal

A.15. Guarding the mountains—Nuba SPLA soldiers.
(*Julie Flint, 1995*)

A.16. New recruits at SPLA training camp.
(*Julie Flint, 1995*)

A.17. Yousif Kuwa Mekki receives a blessing from a Kujur (traditional healer). (*Julie Flint, 1995*)

A.18. Yousif Kuwa.
(*Julie Flint, 1995*)

4

"Things were no Longer the Same"

The Story of Yousif Kuwa Mekki in his Own Words

My mother is Zeinab Somi Tutu. My father is Kuwa Mekki. He used to be a soldier. During the colonial days of course they used to take the youths from the Nuba Mountains, to recruit them as soldiers, especially during the Second World War. My father fought in Ethiopia, actually in Eritrea, in Keren, then he was taken to el Alamein, in the west of Sahara, then he fought there, then after the end of the war they were brought back. Also they were used to fight the rebellious Nubas in the Nuba Mountain. My mother told me I was born when my father came from the fight in Tullishi. That was in 1945, which is why I believe I was born at that time. The second thing she told me, was that it was during the middle of the rainy season, and that could be August. So I was born in August in 1945, but of course I cannot remember the day.

We were five boys and two girls. My mother gave birth to nine children. Two of them died and we remained seven. I was born in a place in Miri district in a place called al Akhwal. There is a hill called al Akhwal. We don't know if the hill takes the name from the people or the people take the name from the hill. So al Akhwal is a hill, and the tribe there are called al Akhwal—you never know who took the name from the other. So when you talk about Limon, you are talking of the people of Limon, in the mountain of Limon. This is in the Nuba Mountains.

My parents were Miri. I am number one, the first-born, and of course in the Nuba Mountains we give the name according to the number you are born. If you are a number one boy, you are Kuku, and a girl is Kaka...

I think Islam came during the time of our grandfather. Mekki is an

Arabic name. I don't know his Nuba name. But strangely enough my father was called Haroun, but then when he was taken as a soldier, he just dropped Haroun and said, "Why should I use it, I should be Kuwa." So he took his name as Kuwa. And he came and gave me this Arabic name, Yousif. At the beginning he wanted to call me Mohamed. But my mother did not become pregnant after a long time, and they went to visit the grave of one of the fakis, they asked through him that the mother should become pregnant. After that it happened that she became pregnant, so instead of Mohamed they called me Yousif. This is the story my father told me. That holy man whom my father visited with my mother was called Yousif Abu Shara. Even up to now, my aunt used to call me Abu Shara, Yousif Abu Shara.

We were taken as children to the schools. It is very interesting to explain when I started my rebellion. It is when I was in elementary school. I think I was in grade four. There was a headmaster. Of course he came from the North. And he was always saying, "Why should these Nuba boys be taught, they should go to work as servants in the houses," or whatever. Because truly the majority of our people used to go to the North and most of them worked in the houses as servants and in such types of bad jobs. So he was often saying, "Why should the Nuba boys be taught?" The worst part of it I remember was that when the bell used to ring for the start of the lessons, this headmaster used to come and sit under the tree, while he was supposed to be teaching us. He used to come rarely, and most of the time he would sit under the tree, or do what he wanted, without teaching us. Of course, this made us unhappy about him and the way he used to insult the Nuba people and so on.

One day, he said, "Why should I teach these Nuba boys?" It happened that I was hearing all that he was saying. There was a rule in the school, whenever you are sitting down and the headmaster or one of the teachers comes, all the students have to stand up, of course like our masters the British, when they were our colonizers. The next day when the headmaster came I remember we were sitting on those benches, all the students stood up except myself. I refused to stand up having in mind the insult I heard the previous day. So, the headmaster called me: "Yousif, come here!" So I rushed to him. "Are you sick?" he asked. "No," I replied. "Why didn't you stand up?" he asked. I kept silent. He then looked at me and told me to go. He didn't punish me. So, I think this was my first rebellion.

At school, of course we were taught in Arabic. One of the things I still remember very well was that when we were taken to school at that time we were told not to speak in our mother tongue and we used to be punished if were found to be talking in our mother tongue. So we started of course to learn the Arabic culture.

When we were in the Nuba Mountains in that time my father was a soldier in the Sudan Army. He was stationed in Malakal, I remember, when for the first time we sat for exams for the intermediate level. I started my primary school at Miri Juwa. And then we were taken to Dilling to sit for the exams. With the type of headmaster who used not to give lessons, you couldn't expect anybody to pass the exams. So actually that is what had happened—from the whole school nobody passed that exam. I then took a lorry from Kadugli via al-Liri and Tonga and from there to Malakal to where my father was.

When I arrived there I found them going back to the North. Soldiers used to be brought to the South for two years and then sent back again to the North and so on. That was the time of Anyanya. So when I went there I found my father was being sent to Eastern Sudan. So I went with him to a place called Jobait, which was then their headquarters, and I repeated the school year there. And I then sat the exams there and I was accepted in Sinkat intermediate school. The school at that time was not built, so we went to Kassala intermediate school for two years. After that we came back to Sinkat after the school was built and we finished the intermediate level there.

Well at that time every thing was going very smoothly, I don't remember anything in the intermediate school, with the exception of when we were in Sinkat, the teachers were very good teachers and we were always in competition with Kassala school. And I remember our class used to be better than the other classes. The teachers would always appreciate our class. And I remember I was one of those who were very good in mathematics. So whenever any class used to have a problem in maths, one of us used to be called, we were three at that time in our class, to humiliate the other class. "You come and solve this problem", the teacher would say. The teacher would always insult Kassala students by saying, "Look here are the students". This used to make us feel proud when we went back to our class. Anyway, I think the time of the intermediate didn't have any problem with the exception of the feeling of being black, which was a problem there. Because our friends the Hadandawa, if you are black with this curly hair they call you *keeshiab*, which means *abid*, slave in English. And of course that was nothing.

It was when I came to higher secondary school at Khartoum Commercial School that was where things started to change. I remember that during the intermediate school I used to be a very good Moslem, I used to do my prayers especially on Fridays. I would go to the mosque all the time. Even when I came to Khartoum I used to be a good Moslem. But when I went to the second year, I remember an incident that happened which shocked me a great deal. As we know, in Khartoum or in Sudan in general, if you are black you would be called *abid*, slave. Well you can accept it from your colleagues and so on. But when you find the educated people saying the same thing you will feel this bitterness.

I remember the first incident was when he was explaining one of the religious aspects regarding your destiny after death. He said, "When you die, by the time people take you to the grave, if you are a Moslem, two beautiful white angels will come and ask you about your name and your religion and so on. Then they will open a window for you to heaven. But if you are not a Moslem, a black angel with red eyes, an *abid*, will come to you instead." Then I said, without thinking, it was just a reaction: "Even angels, the black ones are slaves!" I said it actually as a response, I didn't even think about it. And this shocked everybody in the class. But nobody uttered a word. The period continued.

Then in 1964, after the October Revolution the women in Sudan were given the right to vote and to be elected as members in the parliament. I remember when Fatima Ahmed Ibrahim was elected at that time; she was the first lady to be elected. When that happened, when that decision was made that the women have rights to vote and to be elected, there was a very tough argument all around. So the Islamic teacher at school came and asked the students their opinion about this saying, "What do you think about women having rights for election?" So the students expressed different views; some were in favour and others were against. I remember I was among those who were in favour of the rights of women, coming from the Nuba Mountains where there is no difference between women and men. Then the teacher was asked to give his views and he said, "Giving women their rights! Women don't work even in their houses: they have the Nuba boys to do the work!" So, I couldn't tolerate that.

Then after some time there came a third incident. That's when things fell apart. After that second incident, as a habit whenever I was not happy, I used to draw. I remember I was in the class and started to draw with the chalk on the desk, and I draw an African head. Of course to draw the hair you have to make dots, which made some noise. At that time that teacher was teaching, while I was completely involved in my drawing and not paying attention. Then suddenly I heard "Yousif Kuwa get out of the class!" I put my things away and went out of the class. And that was the first time in my life to be sent out of a classroom. In fact I used to be a very good student—an ideal student in terms of academics and behaviour—I don't think I used to have a problem with anybody. So when I was told to get out of the class I really felt upset. Then I started to think that he shouldn't have driven me out of the class. But in the end I thought, well I made a mistake and whatever the punishment is, I had to go and apologize to the teacher and to tell him I am sorry and I didn't mean it. So when the bell rang to signal the end of the lessons I went to talk to him to apologize. When he saw me and said to me, "Go away, you are a very bad student." So I thought well, maybe what I said last time was still ringing in his mind, and that is why he was saying this. So I went to the class and did not go to him again. As the previous incident had been the question of the Nuba being the ones working in houses, so I became very angry and took my books and kicked the desk, and said "Why should I stay here then, I should go and work with the Nuba."

And I went out of the class. And I started to question myself and question everything, "What is this Islam?" The only thing I came out with was, that there is God. To me that was a blessing because it pushed me to think instead of taking things as they are. And also this made me to think about the Kujurs and about these traditional African religions and so on. Besides, being insulted as a Nuba this gave me the political awareness, why should the Nuba be the ones do all these bad jobs in Sudan and so on? From there I started to think more than before. Religiously I became a bit of a free-thinker. There came a feeling of disequilibrium concerning the spiritual side of it, until I read a certain book, and I started to feel that, we have our spirituality as Africans.

My first-born son, I called him Nyerere. Because in fact Nyerere is one of the people who really helped me with my way of thinking, especially as an African. He helped me even from the religious point of view. Because as a Moslem, one used to feel unhappy, as if there is something you are not sure about. As Moslems we are told to believe in other things, but as Africans, we have seen other things. We see the kujurs, and people doing things, in front of us. Moslems have to reject these things: this is nonsense. This is *sheitan* or devils and so on. And this creates a conflict within yourself, whether you don't believe what you see with your eyes, things happening and done in front of your eyes. But as a Moslem you are told not to believe it, to reject it as a *sheitan*, and so on. You don't feel satisfied; there is no equilibrium between your beliefs and your soul.

When I came to the university, I read a book by Nyerere called "Let us run while we walk." The point that really relieved me was this. He said, after Tanganiyika's independence, when the Tanganyikans wanted to discriminate against the British, he told the people, "These are our guests, we have to respect them even if they were our colonisers now they are part and parcel of us." He said the western magazines and newspapers appreciated what he did. But when he declared a socialist country, all the same press went back to say, "Oh, Nyerere became red," and so on and so forth. Then he said, "Yes I am a Christian, but I took Christianity after I was twelve years old. Although I am a Christian, I believe as Africans we have our own spirituality which I believe in." And he gave a story. He said his father had many wives. And when one of the wives had to go to a funeral, and his father sent him with her to that funeral, they spent some days there and then they were due to come back. It is a tradition in Africa, when you have a relative leaving, you will give him something to go with, whatever you have. So he said, that woman was given a goat and Nyerere was supposed to take that goat with him. When he tried to take it, the goat pulled him backwards, when he was pulling the other way. So one of his relatives saw them pulling each other, the goat and Nyerere. Then he called, "the goat does not want to go with you? You come." And he took some of his hair, Nyerere's hair, and some of the goat's, well he did something, and then, he said, then the goat followed me up to the house, without any force. He said, let anyone tell me or explain this religiously or scientifically. So Nyerere said, I believe as Africans we have our own spirituality. In fact that point really relieved me. And up to today I feel I do not any longer have that uncertainty of my beliefs. That is why I decided that if I got a boy I would call him Nyerere. And I got that first-born boy, Nyerere, but unfortunately after two and a half years he died. That is my Kuku.

Then in 1964, when for the first time Nuba came together and formed General Union of the Nuba and started to talk about the grievances in the Nuba Mountains, and I became part of that organisation in 1965. After some time I worked as a teacher for seven years and then I came back to the university, where I started to read and develop my thinking. I was in the faculty of economics reading political and social studies. During the intermediate and the secondary school we used to read Arabic literature, where we read things that were not part of us. And then I found the book of Chinua Achebe, "Things Fall Apart", and started to read it. The book started with wrestling and of course wrestling is part of our culture, and when I read this although I was in Khartoum, it was as if I could smell the smells of the mountains and feel as if I were there. Even the culture was the same. For example in Nigeria in each village there is a playground the same as the Nuba Mountains, where from six o'clock you will never find any youth in the house. They all go to the playground to dance and play, especially when there is moonlight.

So after finishing that book, I felt that I had found part of myself in that book. That is when I started to read books of African literature. From there I started to see the difference between being an African and being an Arab, and of course I found myself as an African.

Until the time of secondary school I used to feel that I was an Arab, because I was taught that! This is when I started to think that there is something wrong. When I came to the university I found out that there is something wrong in Sudan that should be corrected. I remember since elementary school until I went to the university, there was nothing in the history books about the Nuba that was good. It was only about how the Turks came to Sudan and brought slaves from the Nuba Mountains and the South. So, in these books, we are always slaves. We didn't read anything that makes us proud of being a Nuba. This is why you find a lot of us Nuba, especially the educated ones, hate themselves for being Nuba. As Moslems, they will hate their culture, and they would like to distance themselves from being Nuba. If you ask one of them, for example: "Who are you?", they will change their names from Kuwa and Tiya into Arabic names. If you also asked them about their places of birth their would tell you they were born in Abbassiya Omdurman or Kosti, or whatever, denying the fact that they came from the Nuba Mountains. Up to now this inferiority complex makes a lot of Nuba feel that they don't belong to the Nuba race. They feel ashamed of what is called "Nuba."

I was one of those people, even until higher secondary school. It was only when the General Union of Nuba started, and it began to make me feel, "Why not, this is me! And I should be proud of myself." One day, during Ramadan, I was fasting, and when you are fasting you don't feel interested in these syllabus books, so you prefer to go and read something more interesting. One day I went to Khartoum library and I started to look into Sudan section, and I asked myself: "Why don't I search about things written about the Nuba?" I went around and found a big book about the Nuba written by Siegfried Nadel, in 1947. From that I started to know about the Nuba and their rich culture. It was very strange for me, because all this time I hadn't known anything about the Nuba, who they are, what are they and so on and so forth. And also I found many books inside that library about the Nuba and their origins. Now came a big question, "Why are we not taught about this in our schools?" It is a good history. You find the Kush Kingdom and great civilisations were established by the Nuba in history.

The conclusion of course was that there is something wrong in Sudan that must be corrected. And this question of Sudan being an Arab country really is the wrong basis on which Sudanism is built. With this in my mind I started to think, we have to do something. I remember in 1977, when we were studying we had a lot of Nuba students at the university, and we made a seminar and we invited those Nuba students who feel that there was a problem with the Nuba. We had a discussion for four days and we came out with a resolution that we have two things that divide people: religion and tribalism. Secondly, in order to serve our people we have to work with the system. That was during Nimieri's time. Most of the Nuba people don't like to deal with politics. So we decided we have to do something, but first let us unite as Nuba. That was the beginning of recruiting the young. We were concentrating on the youth because most of the Nuba youth by then were not part of any political party, therefore they were easily recruited. This is how Komolo came to existence.

At the university there were few of us who were Komolo members, like Abd el-Aziz Adam el-Hilo, Kuku Jagdool, there were others. At the university there used to be the Kordofan Students Union. Later, we had two provinces, South and North Kordofan. So we broke the Kordofan Union into two and we started to work on that. I remember we organised a Nuba week at the university, and it was fantastic, as we brought all types of cultural dances, and even we made a Nuba kitchen where we cooked our baliela and asida and so on. We started to discuss some of the historical things, even the comparison between Nuba and the Nubians in terms of languages. It was very good. Anyway, that was where we started.

I finished university in 1980 and I then worked as a teacher at Kadugli Secondary School for one year, 1981. Then Nimieri announced these regional policies, regional government and regional parliament and so on. Being a graduate with a degree in political science, at that time I had many things in mind to do. But the first thing I thought of was establishing myself and then going to politics. Well, unfortunately after coming from the university I got married in 1980, and marriages are problems.

I was working in Darfur, to help support my family. One of my cousins used to live in El-Dilling, and at the time I used to come from Darfur through El-Dilling to Kadugli. And I used to stay with him sometimes, for two or three days and then proceed to Kadugli. One day, he asked me, why are you staying without a wife? I told him that I didn't want to marry. He said, "No...no!" And he went and mobilised all my sisters to press me, and then he told me that he knew two girls here in El-Dilling, and they are very good girls, they come from the Miri tribe—although they are not pure Miri—and you have to choose one of them. For one year I just sent messages. One day I decided to go and see his offer. So, Fatima happened to be my choice. She didn't say yes immediately, of course—if one of them wants something, she will not say yes. That's why I married her after finishing university.

I taught for one year in Kadugli Secondary School (Tilaw). In the evenings we also used to teach in what was called the "Teachers Union," which were night classes. Of course, that helped me to pay back the money I borrowed for my marriage. As a teacher I didn't have any problem in teaching. I think teaching is a good job and I like it. It was only when this question of the Kordofan Parliament came up that things changed.

I didn't have any idea of contesting for election at that time. But one of the teachers, called Ahmed El-Haj, came to me one day and told me that there was going to be a regional parliament and there would be elections. He said, "I have been thinking all this time and I have come to the conclusion that you are the best one who can contest these elections." He told me that, the Nuba here are divided into camps, Mahmoud Hassieb's camp, who used to be the commissioner, in addition to Abd al-Rahman Idris camp. So whenever one of the camps decided to contest an election, several ones from the other side would try to contest as well. So, at the end the gainers will be only the Jallaba in Kadugli—whenever there are elections, the Nuba vote is divided and nobody from the Nuba will win. He told me, "You have been outside all this time (because I used to teach in Darfur) you are not part of any party, so I think you are the right person to go for the elections." I told him frankly, that since my graduation, I have these political ideas in my head, which I would like to put into practice, but I cannot go for elections now, because I didn't have any money. Then he said, "Well, who from the Nuba here has money? If we don't have money does that mean we will surrender and give the chance to the Jallaba to decide our fate?" Anyway we discussed the issue and he convinced me to stand for the elections.

Next, I went to the Komolo members. Ahmed El-Haj himself was a Komolo member. I told them about what happened and asked them about their opinion. I asked how we can succeed, bearing in mind the fact that we don't have money and we don't have any resources. They said, "No, we will do it, whatever we have we will do it." Well, then we started. I remember I went to Khartoum to get some money from our colleagues there who used to be at the university, ten pounds from this one, five pounds from that one, and so on, to come and pay for the campaign. Anyway, this is how I started. I even used to walk or ride a bicycle to contact the people. But in the end I won the elections.

Of course the Jallaba in Kadugli had all the resources. They used to have cars. I just had a bicycle. So, I went around telling people that I was intending to stand for election. But I told them frankly, "I have no money, and you know that my father didn't have money and I am only a teacher, but I think I can represent you and I can talk on your behalf." But, what we agreed to do is this: we said to them, "If the Jallaba come, don't say no, they will try to form a committee including you, agree to that. They will tell you to swear, you swear, and if you swear then you can give your vote to them, but in place of your vote we need ten votes. You have to tell ten people to vote for us, this is one. Secondly the Jallaba will give you money: you take that money, but you should ask them to bring a car. If the car is brought, you would be the ones who are going around with that car, or at least one of you. They will put their symbols on that car, but don't involve yourselves in what's happening inside the car." And this is exactly what had happened, their cars were full with our people, taking them from anywhere to the ballot boxes. It was a tough competition. We were ten candidates in number, eight of them were Nuba boys, and all the attempts to get them to withdraw in favour of one Nuba candidate were rejected. So, we were eight Nuba with two Jallaba. The real competition was between three of us, two of the Jallaba and myself. This is really how we succeeded and it was a shock for the Jallaba. From then on our Nuba people started to have confidence in themselves. I think the problem for the Jallaba was that they believed in their money rather than anything else, otherwise they would have evaluated that things were no longer the same.

5

Focus on Crisis in the Nuba Mountains

Suleiman Musa Rahhal

The Beginning of the Conflict

The war started in the Nuba Mountains in 1985. Until that point, South Kordofan was a peaceful and tranquil area. Relations between the Nuba and the Arabs of South Kordofan were generally good despite minor clashes over cattle grazing and water holes that were usually settled peacefully. But when war came to the area, the situation was completely changed. Latent conflicts exploded into violence. The whole history of conflict and oppression in the Nuba Mountains took on a new meaning, as Nuba youths took up arms to defend their communities.

The history of conflict in the Nuba Mountains goes back to Turco-Egyptian rule in the Sudan in 1821-1885. When the Egyptian ruler Mohammed Ali Pasha conquered Sudan, one of his two main objectives was to recruit black slaves to reinforce his empire-building army. This was the beginning of the slave trade in the Sudan and centred on the Nuba Mountains, Southern Blue Nile and the South. For several decades thereafter, the Turks, private entrepreneurs and Arab traders from northern Sudan raided these areas for slaves.

During the reign of the Khalifa Abdallahi Ta'aishi, who succeeded al-Mahdi in 1885, the situation for the Nuba worsened. Under his regime, the Nuba were cruelly treated. Their villages were raided, tens of thousands of civilians were massacred and a large number were carried off as slaves to Omdurman.

The Nuba resisted British colonisation in the early years of the 20th century. There were repeated rebellions against imperial rule by local Nuba leaders, which were put down by punitive missions that in at least one case involved aerial bombardment. Nuba resistance ceased in the 1920s, after which the area was peaceful, but neglected and cut off from the main social and economic development of Sudan on account of the Closed District ordnance. Government schools in the area were few and late. Only a few mission schools were present to educate a whole generation of Nuba youth.

The Nuba's political struggle in Sudan goes back as far as 1938, when a Nuba political consciousness first started to emerge. This commenced with the formation of 'al Kutla al-Sawda'—the Black Bloc—uniting the people of the Nuba Mountains, Darfur and West Africa. This first black political movement was formed by Dr. Adam Adham, a Darfurian who asked why economic, social and political power should be in the hands of the northern Arab elite alone. One of the main objectives of the Black Bloc was to strive for recognition of the rights of all Sudanese and to ensure that power should never be handed over to the Arabs, who had within living memory been their slave masters.

It was a daunting and frustrating task for the Black Bloc to succeed as a political organisation. Both the Umma and Democratic Unionist Parties opposed the registration of the Black Bloc, accusing the organisation of being racist. The two main parties put pressure on the British Administration not to register it, and they succeeded. The British gave in and refused to register the Black Bloc as a political organisation.

This frustrating moment for the Nuba turned into a political dilemma with far-reaching consequences for their political future. As a result of the banning of the Black Bloc, Nuba were not given the right of representation in the House of Representatives of 1953-1955. The people of the South were in a better situation than the Nuba as they had fifteen MPs in the House of Representatives and were promised a federation for the South if they voted for a united Sudan. Southerners, however, later came to realise that they had been cheated, as they were not included in the delegations sent to Egypt for the critical Cairo Conference on the future of the Sudan.

This omission led to frustration and deep resentment among the people of Southern Sudan as well as among the people of the Nuba Mountains. This frustration in turn developed into an armed struggle in the South even before independence. As for the Nuba people, their political movement went underground while at the same time working openly under the umbrella of social organisations in the Nuba Mountains area and Khartoum.

The first national government of Ismail al-Azhari drew up an education policy based on the Arabization of the entire country. The use of local languages was forbidden in the Nuba Mountains, the South, Darfur and the Ingessena Hills. Children in the Nuba Mountains were not allowed to attend school unless they adopted Arabic names. General Ibrahim Aboud, who took power in a military coup in 1958, pursued the same policy but with greater determination. It was by now evident that the Northern politicians were working on a hidden agenda of assimilation and suppression of non-Arab

Sudanese

Father Philip Abbas Ghaboush, a former Anglican clergyman, was chosen as first leader of the GUNM. The main objectives of the organisation were:

1. To call for the unity of the Nuba
2. To revive the Nuba Mountains Province
3. To abolish poll tax
4. To establish an educational programme for the region
5. To get parliamentary representation for the Nuba people
6. To implement an acceptable solution to the Southern question
7. To enforce a policy of Africanising Sudan rather than Arabising it with the eventual aim of black rule over the whole country.

The Nuba found these objectives appealing and rallied behind Ghaboush. To bring this programme about, the United Sudanese African Liberation Front uniting the Nuba and other non-Arab groups planned a coup against Mohammed Ahmed Mahgoub for 29 May 1969, but it was pre-empted by Numieri on 25 May.

During the spells of democratic government, the people of the Nuba Mountains, the Beja Hills and Darfur were politically undermined and marginalised by the two main parties despite the strong showing of regional parties in the 1965 elections. The regional parties entered Parliament with great hopes that they could gain better conditions for their regions, but saw their hopes drain away. The periods of so-called democratic government turned out to be the more disastrous than military dictatorship for the people of the regions. These governments appeared to have no direction for the country, no management of any kind and were bedevilled by the corruption of senior ministers. As a result, the regions were neglected while an accelerated rate of development in northern Sudan led to greater exploitation of young Nuba migrants who had no recourse against racial discrimination.

It was only a matter of time before the Nuba would turn to armed struggle to defend their co-existence, their political rights and their cultural identity. When the Sudan People's Liberation Movement (SPLM) produced a manifesto declaring a revolutionary struggle for the sake of creating a "New Sudan" based on equality, power-sharing and justice, a significant number of Nuba joined the SPLA movement. Yousif Kuwa Mekki, a graduate of Khartoum University, was among the first Nuba to join the movement, becoming first commander of the New Kush Battalion and latterly a senior SPLA commander and Governor of South Kordofan.

The Nuba people's relations with the south only started to develop in recent years. In the past, the people of Nuba Mountains and Darfur formed the bulk of the rank-and-file of the Sudanese armed forces used to prosecute the civil war in the south. This was a central policy of all governments based on divide-and-rule tactics. Today the relationship between the people of Nuba Mountains and the South is strong and has been moulded into a fighting alliance. The two peoples have similar grievances from injustices inflicted on them for generations by tyranny in Khartoum. Both are marginalised in Sudanese society.

In the wake of the Popular Uprising against President Nimeiri in April 1985, the transitional government of Major General Sowar al-Dahab took power and betrayed the promise of peace. In fact, the Transitional Military Council intensified the existing imbalance of power between Arabs and Nuba, and began to arm the Baggara Arab tribes. The government of Sadig al-Mahdi followed the same policy on taking office in April 1986 and, under Defence Minister Fadlallah Burma, gave even more sophisticated weapons to the Baggara Arabs, especially the Misseriya. Neighbouring Baggara tribes became confident and, armed with their new Kalashnikov rifles, raided and looted villages, destroyed Nuba properties and committed massacres.

The conflict in the Nuba Mountains intensified further when Lieutenant General Omer al-Bashir seized power in June 1989. Backed by the National Islamic Front (NIF), Bashir's military regime continued the policies already mapped out by the Sadig al-Mahdi government but expanding them in an attempt to eradicate Nuba identity and culture. On the pretext of fighting the Sudan People's Liberation Army (SPLA), a fatwa-or Islamic decree-was issued declaring a Jihad (Holy War) against the Nuba people. But this was more than a war of religion. It was a war for the rich and natural resources of the Nuba Mountains fuelled by the question of ethnic rights and the ready availability of modern weapons.

The Jihad in the Nuba Mountains has destroyed the entire infrastructure of Nuba society. Grave human rights violations that continue to this day, rape, child abduction and mass killing, add up to a crime of genocidal proportions against the Nuba people. This chapter charts some of the dimensions of the war and associated its atrocities.[1]

The Collapse into Conflict

Many generations of Nuba have shared the rich land of South Kordofan with nomadic Baggara Arabs, the Messiriya Humur and Hawazma, who migrated to the area with their cattle and settled on the plains among the Nuba. Other also inhabits the area, smaller groups including the Jellaba (Arab merchants from the North) and the Fellata who migrated from West Africa in the past 300 to 400 years.[2]

Earlier this century, the Nuba resolved their disputes with their neighbours after years of slavery and raiding and began living side by side in relative peace. Over the years, relations between the two communities developed into mutual trust, with inter-marriage and cultural exchange. Both Nuba chiefs and Arab sheikhs were wise enough to resolve their disputes without resorting to violence, helped by customary laws, which had more respect for the individual than today's civil laws.

After the Mahdiya era, large numbers of Arabs converged on Kadugli where they petitioned the Nuba king, Mek Rahhal, for land. Some of them, the ones who wrote Quranic verses, were given a place near the Mek and called "Hellat al-Fougara" after them. Another group was given a place at al-Shair, ten miles north of Kadugli, which is now a centre of activities for Popular Defence Force (PDF). Others were given land too, and became loyal to the meks and chiefs. Mek Rahhal trusted these Arabs to the extent that he chose two of them as members of his court, where they became advisors, and referred to them as wise men. Land and water disputes were resolved in annual conferences attended by all Nuba meks and chiefs and by Arab nazirs and sheikhs. These meetings customarily took place on neutral ground at a place called Kaylak.

In some areas, Nuba converted to Islam out of respect for the wisdom of Arab sheikhs. In others, the spread of Islam was strongly resisted. Today in the Nuba Mountains almost half the Nuba practise Islam and the majority speak Arabic. Before war came to the mountains, Islam, Christianity and local beliefs were practised side by side without prejudice or pressure, creating a remarkable religious tolerance among the Nuba. It was common to find more than one religion in a single family. But this religious freedom ended with the coming to power of the National Islamic Front (NIF), which is attempting to Islamise the whole of Sudan through repression and coercion while harbouring ambitions of spreading its Islamic revolution to neighbouring countries as well.

Under laws first laid down by the Anglo-Egyptian condominium, nomads were not allowed to enter the agricultural areas of the Nuba Mountains before crops were harvested. In more recent years, conflicts over land disputes, grazing and water-holes have meant that these laws are no longer implemented and clashes have broken out between Nuba farmers and Arab herdsmen, accelerating the breakdown of relations.

The 1970s marked the beginning of drastic deterioration in the Nuba Mountains—with the sole exception of the period 1974-79 in which Mahmoud Hasseib, himself a Nuba, served as Commissioner of South Kordofan. Hasseib succeeded in reducing Arab-Nuba tension and giving the Nuba confidence. For the first time, the area witnessed positive developments that encouraged many educated Nuba to return to contribute to the process of development. Hasseib's term of office, however, was cut short when he was shot dead at close range in his office by a gunman. Though the killer was brought to justice, many Nuba believed this was a political assassination. Some believe that this has to do with his nomination for post of Governor of Kordofan which cost him his life. After his death the relations between the two communities began to disintegrate and deteriorated badly.

Following the overthrow of Field-Marshal Gaafar Nimeiri in April 1985, the Nuba-Arab conflict intensified and entered a new phase of hatred and hostility. The transitional government of Sowar al-Dahab began arming the Arab militias, ostensibly to protect their interests in the area against the SPLA, which had made its first incursion into the mountains at al-Gardoud in 1985.

This event lit the spark of war in the Nuba Mountains. The government blames the SPLA for its "invasion" of South Kordofan and the killing of over one hundred Arabs, both militiamen and civilians. This ignores the way in which repression in the Nuba Mountains was already sparking resistance. Hundreds of Nuba youth had already joined the SPLA, following the example of Yousif Kuwa Mekki. Also, the government response to the incursion was savage and disproportionate. It began to create militias from among the Baggara Arabs of South Kordofan and South Darfur.

Known as Murahaliin or Marahil, these militias are drawn from the nomadic Arab tribes who usually move along the grazing belt situated between South Darfur, South Kordofan and Bahr al-Ghazal. They are loyal to Mahdi family and support the Umma Party, to the extent that some of them went to Libya with Sadig al-Mahdi in 1970 and received military training as part of the Ansar military force, and only returned to Sudan after the reconciliation between President Nimeiri and Sadig al-Mahdi in 1978. Many of the returning Ansar settled in South Kordofan.

The U.S. oil company Chevron also played a part in arming the Murahaliin. With the knowledge and support of President Nimeiri, it distributed weapons to the Arabs in order to defend its oilfields from attack by the SPLA. But instead of engaging the SPLA, many Murahaliin went their own way with cattle raids into Dinka and Nuba areas.

When the government of Sadiq al-Mahdi took office in 1986, it also armed the militias. Under the guiding hand of Defence Minister Fadlalla Burma, a Messeriya Arab, the government turned a deaf ear to the protests of Nuba politicians and intellectuals as well as moderate Sudanese outside the Nuba Mountains.

Today the conflict between Arab and Nuba has reached unprecedented levels and seems set to continue for many years to come. There are, however, some positive indications emerging from the Messeriyia Arabs who have come to realise that the Khartoum government has used them in their war with the Nuba and are now seeking to make peace with the Nuba, realising that their interests lie with their neighbours and not with Khartoum.

Root Causes of the Conflict

Although the al-Gardoud massacre ignited the situation, it cannot be considered the root cause of the war in the mountains. Throughout their history, the Nuba people have been cheated of peace. They suffered at the hands of Arab slave traders and during the Mahdiya. Every government that has ruled Sudan since independence has suppressed and marginalized the Nuba. Today the Nuba are confronted with a full-frontal attack against their culture and identity.

The conflict in the Nuba Mountains cannot be separated from the long-standing conflict in the wider Sudan. The Nuba are central to that conflict, having pursued the armed struggle side by side with the SPLA for more than ten years. Today, Nuba are central in this conflict in many ways. They hold the key to the vital questions of land, ethnic rights, and religious tolerance. These are the core elements to the conflict in Sudan today, which need to be addressed for the benefit of the whole country. Therefore the rights of the Nuba people can no longer be ignored or compromised.

It is often said that the underlying cause of the conflict in Sudan is religion. Religion is an element, but it is just one of many factors which have contributed to the conflict over the years.

The Religious Factor

While most Sudanese are Moslems, they are neither extremists nor fanatics. They are simply devout. Yet Islam has been used for many years by the northern political parties, and more recently by the NIF, as a vehicle for gaining political power and imposing an Islamic-Arabic culture on the entire country regardless. Some Northern Sudanese believe Islam is only religion and it is the best culture for all human beings. In an interview for a BBC television documentary in 1983, the governor of Kordofan said: 'From the Islamic point of view, Nuba culture is very ugly and must be eradicated.' He was shown providing clothing to naked Nuba.

The people of Sudan have historically shown a remarkable degree of religious tolerance, especially in the Nuba Mountains, where more than one religion is commonly practised within a single family. What we are experiencing today is an abuse of Islam for economic and political gain far removed from true Islamic values. Religion has become a Trojan Horse for extremists. Signs of religious intolerance have emerged even among the Nuba. In 1994, disturbed by the influence of Khartoum's intolerance, the Nuba in the SPLM-administered areas convened a Religious Tolerance Conference that went a long way towards restoring their traditional harmony. But today they face a new wave of religious intolerance from another quarter: fundamentalist Christian missionaries who are rewarding belief with humanitarian aid, and creating divisions among the Nuba people.

It is one of the many inconsistencies of Sudan's war that its so-called Islamic government is today torturing and killing Nuba Moslems as well as Christians and non-believers, confirming many Nuba in the belief that the war contains a racial element. Arab militias shouting, "Burn the mosques of the slaves" have destroyed Nuba mosques and copies of the Quran. "The enemy has no religion," one Nuba said in testimony to African Rights. "They are burning our mosques and Quran and even killing our Imams." [3]

The Racial Factor

Racial discrimination is a sensitive issue in the Sudan. The word "abid", which means slave and was introduced by the first Arab generation to enter Sudan in the 15-16th century, is widely used to describe non-Arab groups in the Sudan. On some occasions it is used deliberately to degrade and humiliate non-Arabs.

The Nuba have suffered from the policies of both British imperialists and post-independence governments. The "Closed District" policy was implemented from the 1920s to segregate Arabs from Nuba and Southerners in an attempt to protect the latters' cultures and identities. This may have helped preserve traditional Nuba cultures, but the Nuba were denied access to education; administration and development while the Arab in the North were better off. This policy opened up a gap between the people of the north and the people of the peripheries, which eventually contributed to the civil conflict which has torn apart the Sudan for most of the 45 years. When the Riverain Arabs took up power from the British they pursued a policy of "divide and rule" and hitting "slave by slave", particular using Nuba and the people of Darfur in their war against the people of South. The non-Arab groups began to envisage the racial discrimination in many ways and the racial conflict becomes apparent. Today, it is becoming clear that the current civil war in Sudan is not only about sharing of power, economic development but it is also about cultural identity: should the Sudan be an Arab or an African country?

Power-sharing

The concentration of political power and economic development in the hands of the northern Arab elite has played a significant part in contributing to today's civil war. The resentment and frustration caused among the people of the marginalised regions convinced many that armed struggle was the only way to end northern domination and achieve their political objectives.

Northern politicians, whether the sectarian Umma Party, the Democratic Unionist Party (DUP) or the ideologically-based Communist Party and NIF, have all espoused a similar political agenda for the Nuba people. Overtly, all speak about the equality of all Sudanese citizens, but their policies are designed to keep non-riverain people weak and divided. The Nuba have never benefited from any policies to enable them to catch up on the education gap. Nuba farmers are vulnerable to well-financed and well-connected businessmen, civil servants and military officers from northern Sudan who come and buy up their land at cheap prices, and then drive them off. Nuba cultures cannot withstand the onslaught of Arab-Islamic culture in the media, the schools, government offices, market places and mosques. These practices have fuelled tensions that already existed before independence in 1956. It has been all too apparent to the Nuba and the others that they are seen as second-class citizens in their own country.

Until 1964, the Nuba Mountains were dominated politically by the Umma and DUP. These two parties won most of the parliamentary seats in every election, leaving the Nuba with no representation in the constituent assembly in Khartoum. It was only in 1964 that this domination began to diminish due to the formation of the General Union of the Nuba Mountains (GUNM). The newly formed Sudan National Party (SNP) played a similar role in 1986. The emergence of these two Nuba political movements gave a clear signal that the Nuba were capable of representing themselves and running their own affairs. In the elections of 1965 and 1986, the Nuba parties won the majority of the parliamentary seats in the Nuba Mountains. As well as winning all Nuba seats but one in the 1986 election, the biggest shock for the main parties was the victory of Reverend Philip Ghaboush in Khartoum North where he beat the candidates of the NIF, DUP and Umma in their heartland.

1986 was a milestone in Nuba political history and gave the Nuba people a boost, encouragement and greater confidence. The SNP leader, Father Ghaboush, together with the leaders of the other regional parties with African rather than Arab roots combined to form a political alliance called the "Black Bloc." This new African alliance caused great concern among many Northern politicians, and, while the Nuba and others sought to convert their political representation into political power, the big parties set about destroying the Black Bloc and its leader. The conspiracy was largely successful in destroying Nuba aspirations.

Under Prime Minister al-Sadig al-Mahdi, the coalition government of the Umma Party and the DUP drew up a secret agenda for the Nuba Mountains and Darfur region with the intent of destroying the Nuba political parties and the Black Bloc. This involved the gradual removal of Nuba magistrates, senior government officials, senior police and army officers, clerks and teachers and replacing them with Arab personnel, loyal to the Umma Party in particular. The plan was to place local administrative control in the hands of the Baggara tribes in order to ensure the domination of the traditional sectarian parties in the Nuba Mountains and Darfur.

At the same time, the Baggara were given the green light to carry out their own agenda: to drive the Nuba out of the fertile land of the Nuba mountains. The main objectives were:

1. Halt all economic development in black areas and divert future development to areas occupied by Arab tribes.
2. Run down the services in the regions that are occupied by black Sudanese.
3. Destabilise the region, causing political unrest, creating conflict and confusion among non-Arab groups.
4. Block promotions of blacks in South Kordofan and elsewhere.

The plan, entrusted to the newly formed Arab Grouping Movement in south Kordofan and Darfur, was to be enforced by the Arab militias in the knowledge that they would not hesitate to raid, loot and spread terror.

Lack of Economic Development

One of the contributing factors to the conflict is the lack of development in the Nuba Mountains, which have never shared in Sudan's economic development. The Nuba region has been deliberately starved of every kind of development. The schools are poor. Communications are woeful. There are virtually no government health or social services.

Yet the Nuba Mountains are one of the richest regions of Sudan with minerals, fertile soil and great potential for agricultural development. This very richness has been a cause of conflict. In the mid-1970s, the discovery of oil, the rich fertile land of the Nuba and the availability of loan from the World Bank opened up the Nuba Mountains area and encouraged many outsiders to come to the area. The Kordofan regional administration added fuel to the fire by evicting Nuba landowners and allowing Arabs to create huge mechanised farms.

It was policies like these that drove the Nuba within the armed services to revolt against the government in Khartoum. An attempted coup including two Nubas—Abdel Rahman Shambi and Abbas Bersham—in 1976 reflected the discontent and the frustration of the Nuba with the government's political and developmental orientation.[4]

Modern Weapons

Conflicts fought with sticks and spears, perhaps with one or two bolt-action rifles or shotguns, cause few casualties. Traditional methods of conflict resolution, which include paying compensation for the homicides committed and property destroyed, can usually find solutions to such disputes. But the arrival of automatic weapons in the late 1970s changed the balance of power. In the hands of ruthless young men, directed by politicians with wider agendas, the capacity for mass murder became infinitely greater.

The availability of modern weaponry such as the Kalashinkov rifle played its role in encouraging the Murahaliin to raid Nuba villages and terrorise whole areas and eventually gave them the upper hand in the region. By 1989 the SPLA had acquired comparable firepower from its new battalions, graduating from the training camps in Ethiopia, and the war was intense.

Land Sequestration

In the early 1970s it was thought that Sudan could be the bread-basket of the Arab world, making use of the freely available petrodollar loans to expand mechanised farming from the irrigated lands along the Nile westwards into the fertile rain-fed plains of South Kordofan.[5] This idea was encouraged and supported by the World Bank, which supported the creation of the government's Mechanised Farming Corporation (MFC). The introduction of MFC projects on the Nuba Mountains plains had a disastrous effect on the Nuba. Their land was seized, and they were evicted and driven from their ancestral land without compensation.

The hunger for Nuba land not only brought suffering to the Nuba people. It caused widespread environmental and ecological disaster to the region as a result of the clearing of forests, intensive ploughing for quick profit and lack of long-term investment. The environmental decay that has scarred so much of north Kordofan was spreading south, creating further social dislocation and conflict over diminishing resources. Arab herders lost their best pastures as well, and brought their animals onto Nuba smallholdings in search of grass-unlike the big commercial farmers, Nuba villagers had no weapons or hired guards to defend their property.

Mechanised farming grew rapidly. Licensed projects grew from less than half a million hectares in 1968 to some five millions hectares by 1986.[6] Under the present regime of General al-Bashir, the Nuba land given over to mechanised farming has tripled. Most of the fertile land in the eastern part of the Nuba Mountains has been allocated to commercial farmers, including PDF leaders. Many Nuba have become impoverished wage labourers on the farms of absentee landlords and the sustainable agriculture of the Nuba has been replaced by over-intensive farming of thin soil.[7]

Protest is not tolerated. In Mungeinis in Rashad district in 1984, more than eighty Nuba refused to hand their lands to a company formed by rich merchants and government ministers. They were rounded up and after being brought before an emergency court in Kadugli were flogged and imprisoned. Similar cases were reported in the Heiban area. Under the current regime, the entire Nuba population of Abu Jonok was forcibly removed to al-Sount area and Messeriyia nomads settled in their place. At a meeting in London in January 1993, the minister for planning, Dr. Ali al-Haj, declared that his government had made 40,000 feddans available for sale in the Nuba Mountains and Blue Nile region. In the same month, the government announced a programme of land sale in

South Kordofan. The area of Khor Shalngo near Lagowa was sold off-as usual to those with government connections.

In another disturbing policy, the government encouraged the Fellata, people of West African origin, to settle in South Kordofan. The Fellata have long sought their own "homeland" within Sudan, and the current government has not hesitated to exploit them as political supporters, giving them key positions in the administration and security, and rewarding them with land. This is certain to develop into a serious conflict between these two communities, particularly when it comes to whom the land belongs.[8] Similar plans for settling the Fellata in the Southern Blue Nile region caused much local conflict in 1996.

Human Rights Violations

Since the outbreak of the war in the Nuba Mountains in July 1985, there have been serious human rights violations in the Nuba Mountains. During the "democratic" period, 1986-89, security officers in Kadugli, Heiban and other towns detained, tortured and killed dozens of Nuba who were suspected of sympathising with the SPLA. The Arab militias-and after 1987, increasingly the regular army as well were unleashed on defenceless Nuba villages.

When the present NIF government seized power in 1989, the Nuba people had hope of change and sent messages of support to the President and his national security advisor Ibrahim Nayil Idam, himself of Nuba descent. They called upon the government to provide protection for them from the Arab militias. However, the government never came to their aid. Instead, it gave the militias even more freedom and weaponry to drive the Nuba from their land, and the systematic nature of the violations under the NIF regime against the Nuba reached unprecedented scale. To the dismay of the Nuba, one of the first actions of the new government was to pass the Popular Defence Act, which formally recognised the militias as part of the Popular Defence Forces.

In October 1990, the government decided to seal off the South Kordofan area and the Nuba Mountains have ever since been cut off from the rest of the world, besieged by government forces. Military intelligence has detained large numbers of educated Nuba on suspicion of being SPLA sympathisers and for fear that they might act as leaders of their community.[9] Over a hundred Nuba people have been arrested in Kadugli, Dilling, Lagowa and other towns in the Nuba Mountains, subjected to torture and extra-judicial killings.

In a press conference in the Swiss city of Berne in 1993, after defecting to the West, Lieutenant Khalid Abdel Karim Salih, brother of the governor of Kordofan and a security officer in South Kordofan, said publicly that the government was pursuing a policy of ethnic cleansing in the Nuba Mountains.[10] He estimated the number of

Nuba killed in military operations and indiscriminate shelling at 60-70,000. Since then, the government's campaign of ethnic cleansing has been documented by human rights organisations including Amnesty International[11], Africa Watch[12] and most thoroughly by African Rights[13].

From September 1989 to February 1990, the government pursed its campaign of eradicating the Nuba with absolute impunity. Numerous villages were razed to the ground and large numbers of people were killed. The worst massacre occurred near Lagowa in October 1989, when local militias slaughtered more than a hundred Nuba civilians. The entire populations of Lagori and Sabori near Kadugli were massacred when they were called to a meeting by PDF forces disguised as soldiers and claiming to be offering protection. But this was only a foretaste of the assaults that were still to come.

The Jihad against the Nuba

In January 1992, the governor of Kordofan, Abdel Karim al-Husseini, declared a Jihad in the Nuba Mountains. Large number of armed forces including Mujahadiin and Arab militias were sent to the Nuba Mountains. Backed by indiscriminate aerial bombing and shelling, the army destroyed villages, looted, abducted women and children, killed tens of thousands of men and women and displaced hundreds of thousands of Nuba—forcing more than a hundred thousand into camps on the outskirts of Kadugli, Dilling and Lagowa as a prelude to resettlement in so-called "peace camps" in North Kordofan. Many died in these camps from hunger, disease and exposure. Others were forced to work as unpaid labourers on the farms of wealthy Arab merchants.

There are simple answers as to why the NIF government launched its Jihad, even though nearly half the population of the mountains is Moslem, and why it has devoted so much energy to the destruction of Nuba culture and identity.

The regime is intolerant of any culture or beliefs other than its own variant of Islamic and Arabic culture. The NIF government seeks to Islamize all Sudanese in order to form the first Islamic state south of the Sahara as a springboard for spreading Islam to the rest of the continent. The Nuba's strong separate identity is a major obstacle to this project.

On 27 April 1992, a *fatwa*, or religious decree, was issued at an Islamic conference in el-Obeid, the capital of Kordofan. The *fatwa*, signed by five prominent Imams and justified by Koranic verses, was intended to mobilise the masses in northern Sudan and especially in North Kordofan. The *Fatwa* stated that:

The rebels in South Kordofan and Southern Sudan started their rebellion against the state and declared war against Moslems. Their main aims are killing Moslems, desecrating mosques, burning and defiling the Koran, and raping Moslem women. In so doing, they are encouraged by the enemies of Islam and Moslems: these foes are the Zionists, the Christians and the arrogant people who provide them with provisions and arms. Therefore, an insurgent who was previously a Moslem is now an apostate; and a non-Moslem is a non-believer standing as a bulwark against the spread of Islam, and Islam has granted the freedom of killing both of them...

The Jihad campaign unleashed an unprecedented level of military violence in the Nuba Mountains. More than 40,000 troops, supported by tanks, helicopter gun-ships and aircraft, were deployed. The first target was the mountain of Tullishi, where 970 SPLA troops under the command of Alternate Commander Mohamed Juma Nayel were positioned. For four months the government army attacked the mountain, day and night, using all means available to destroy resistance. They failed. In May 1992 Khartoum withdrew its forces, claiming that it had achieved victory—in fact the mountain was still controlled by the SPLA.

Another component of the Jihad campaign was massive forcible resettlement. Part of the plan was to depopulate the Nuba Mountains by moving the Nuba elsewhere. In January 1992, Omer Suleiman Adam, assistant governor for Peace and Rehabilitation affairs in Kordofan, announced that "peace villages" had been prepared for 90,000 "returnees" from the SPLA. The "villages", he said, were part of a project designed to absorb 500,000 people. These "villages" were in the main camps in North Kordofan or on the fringes of mechanised farming schemes on the edges of the mountains, far from the "returnees" homes.[14] By June, 50,000 "returnees" had arrived in Kadugli, Dilling, Telodi and Lagowa. Many were taken out of North Kordofan and relocated in camps around Rahmanyia, south of Rashad.

In September, authorities became concerned with mounting pressure from Nuba groups and foreign governments and began to reduce the numbers being taken from the mountains. But probably the key factor was that by that time, the government's military campaign had been called off in the face of defeats at Tullishi and the eastern mountains. The peak of the genocidal onslaught was over. What followed was a slower, but systematic war aimed at grinding down Nuba resistance- what African Rights called "genocide by attrition."

Extra-Judicial Killings

Immediately following the 1989 military coup, the regime targeted its campaign of eradication on Nuba intellectuals and community leaders in order to silence criticism of its policies. By the middle of 1991 the Nuba Mountains region had witnessed mass detentions of educated Nuba, community leaders and outspoken individuals. Many of the detainees subsequently disappeared without trace.[15]

In September 1991, NMSA received

a report containing a list of 37 educated Nuba detained in Kadugli by the security forces and believed to have been killed in cold blood. Among the confirmed dead were Mohammed Nawar Aso (dentist), Hamdan Kori (lawyer), Yousef Jaldagon (secondary school teacher), Hassan Khir al-Seed (secondary school teacher), Kamal Kano Kafi (radio technician), Tigani Mohammed Shukrallah, Ibrahim Murmaton and al-Sir Abdel Gadir Malik. When relatives of the disappeared asked the authorities in Kadugli for information about their next of kin, they were threatened with a similar fate.

It is believed that the main force behind the disappearances was the former commissioner for South Kordofan, Abdel Wahab Abdel Gadir Rahman, a NIF zealot.[16] In August 1992, Nuba intellectuals in Khartoum met Dr Nafi Ali Nafi, head of security and raised a number of issues including the disappearance of 102 educated Nuba from Kadugli, Dilling and Lagowa. They demanded a public enquiry, which the government refused. Instead, those who attended the meetings were threatened and some later detained.

Human rights violations have proliferated with impunity since the closure of South Kordofan in October 1990. Massacres and mutilation became commonplace between 1990 and 1993. In December 1990 and March 1991, military intelligence in Kadugli embarked on a search for alleged SPLA supporters in the villages of Lagori and Sabori, North-East of Kadugli. Nuba villagers were executed accused of being SPLA sympathisers.

A typical case involved five men arrested in October 1990 in Abu Zabad town and held without trial for thirteen months in al-Obeid prison, during which time they suffered terrible torture. In December 1991, the five: Khalifa Abdel Gadir Karma Allah, a teacher; Ahmed Adam Azrag, Eisa Shareif Adlan and Musa Shareif Adlan, merchants, and Mohammed Humeida Juma' Sa'adan, were handed to military intelligence in the middle of the night and moved to a place near Dilling called Julud. On 4 December, four were shot dead. Juma' Sa'adan, who witnessed the tragedy, managed to escape to an SPLA-controlled area.

In August 1991, Hamza Fargallah was killed by soldiers escorting him from el-Obeid to Lagowa. Another sixteen were arrested, of whom seven were taken to el-Obeid for trial under the state of emergency.[17] Then, in November 1991, NMSA received a report from an eye witness to the killings of more than fifty Nuba from Shatt al-Damam and Katcha, south of Kadugli. They were brought to the military garrison in Dilling where they were executed by firing squad in a single day. On 25 June 1992, after a battle between the SPLA and PDF around al-Fous near Dilling, government forces killed at least sixteen, including two women. Some reports suggest that more than one hundred civilians were killed.[18] In March and April 1993, forty civilians were reportedly extra-judicially executed around Jebel Tabaq. In July, a PDF unit attacked the village of Oma and killed five men and women.[19]

The upsurge in violence continued throughout 1993-94 and in January 1994, 228 civilians were reported killed in Jebel Ashum and 113 in Heiban. Between the end of December 1992 and the beginning of 1993, hundreds of civilians were reported to have been killed at Jebel Heiban and buried in a mass grave.[20]

Shortly before the beginning of 1995, more than 10,000 government and militia troops assembled in Kadugli for the dry season offensive. After a short break over the New Year, attacks continued, and thirteen villages were burned to the south and east of Kadugli. An unknown number of people were killed. Defenceless villages were attacked, grain stores burned, wells poisoned and goats stolen[21]. On 28 March, immediately after the "Guinea worm" ceasefire was announced, the government began transferring forces from the South to the Nuba Mountains and stepped up its military assaults.

This pattern has continued in subsequent years. Usually, during the dry season, the Sudan Government launches an offensive targetted at the major strategic points held by the SPLA in the southern and eastern hills. During the dry months when the terrain is passable for armoured vehicles, the Sudan army has the edge, and can often capture the small towns and villages in the plains. Aerial bombardment unleashed against SPLA bases and civilian villages—and also relief centres and hospitals in the hills—is deployed alongside the ground assault. The armoured columns burn everything they encounter, and round up the inhabitants of the villages at gunpoint to take them to garrisons and "peace villages." During the rainy season, the tables are turned, and government outposts become isolated, vulnerable to guerrilla attacks. During these periods, the government relies increasingly on aerial bombardment, a form of indiscriminate violence that merely kills and terrorises civilians and has no military utility. The other main element in the government's war is crime: it encourages members of the PDF to roam around the countryside in small gangs, terrorising, killing, looting and raping. These PDF elements also plant anti-personnel landmines on paths and around water holes. By these means they are able to create large "no-go" areas in the vicinity of garrisons.

Food as a Weapon of War

The systematic campaign of destruction of Nuba society began immediately after non-governmental organisations working in the mountains were expelled in 1991. After that the government established a blockade on any relief supplies entering the area. This soon became a policy of establishing "peace camps" and aid-supported projects in the main government-controlled towns while preventing any humanitarian assistance reaching contested areas or SPLA-controlled areas. At the same time, local authorities have taken harsh measures to ensure that no medicine or food entered the area. People found carrying food were arrested and the food confiscated. Many were killed for this "offence". Hospitals in the area have been converted into military hospitals. The sick have been denied medication and treatment and sent home to die, accused of being rebels or SPLA sympathisers.

For more than ten years after Operation Lifeline Sudan was established, the Sudan Government completely prevented any official assistance reaching the SPLA-held areas of the Nuba Mountains. In June 1994, NMSA learnt that the government delegation threatened to walk out of a meeting with OLS in Nairobi if the word Nuba was used.

During a visit to Sudan in December 1993, the UN's Special Envoy for Humanitarian Affairs for the Sudan, Ambassador Vieri Traxler, requested permission for the UN and international relief organisations to provide relief for the tens of thousands of civilians in the Nuba Mountains. The government refused. The prevention of food relief has become one of the government's main weapons for depopulating the mountains. It is more effective than bullets, with the starving Nuba forced to choose between death from hunger or life in one of the peace camps.

In the area under government control, food has been used by Islamic NGOs, especially al-Da'wa al-Islamiya, to control and Islamize the Nuba. Those refusing to convert to Islam are denied access to food centres run by Islamic relief agencies. Furthermore, food is used as a magnet to force the Nuba out of SPLA-controlled areas with the promise of food in the so-called "peace camps".

Currently, the government is promoting a policy dubbed "Peace from Within" and has called upon the Nuba people to participate. However, the experience of the Belenga peace talks of 1992, where the Nuba were genuinely ready to make peace with the government but were betrayed, made them to belief that the government is not serious about achieving peace. The Nuba believe that "peace from within" is nothing but a trick to force them to join the PDF and fight their own people.

The 1996 review of Operation Lifeline Sudan revealed the collaboration between the UN and the NIF government in its attempts to use food as a weapon of destruction. The review said UN operations had committed "a fundamental failure to adapt programming to the fact of internal warfare and its associated risks for some populations".

In this regard, it is difficult to understand how humanitarian assistance can be made to contribute to the conflict reduction. UNICEF, for example, is supporting Child Friendly Village schemes in some 29 villages in South Kordofan. The fact that UNICEF is able to support such schemes, in a context where internal warfare has placed children at great risk, led the Review Team to question the extent of UN understanding of realities...[22]

A larger and even more disturbing programme is the UN Development Programme's Area Rehabilitation Scheme centred on Kadugli, the largest town in the Nuba Mountains. The aim of the ARS scheme is to support the government's policy of resettling "returnees" in peace villages. The government claims that agricultural development will strengthen the "returnees" attachment to the land. In reality, however, the government uses the scheme to fund the war in the Nuba Mountains and in the South.

I know what we are doing is supporting a government programme, building up peace villages and supporting the Popular Defence Forces," one aid worker told the review team." There has to be a balance on the other side. We are doing good work, but there are bigger political issues that need addressing.[23]

The review concluded that aid agencies had tolerated abuses against the Nuba by failing to challenge the humanitarian embargo imposed by the government even though the Nuba Mountains fell squarely within the mandate of OLS.

International Responses

In December 1991, Africa Watch published the first report on the war against the Nuba, warning that the Nuba risked the destruction of their ethnic identity and being reduced to a subclass of displaced people.[24] By mid-1992 the human rights crisis in the Nuba Mountains and elsewhere in Sudan had reached an unprecedented scale and drawn the attention of the media as well as international human rights groups.

The first response from the UN came in September 1992, when the UN special envoy, Jan Eliasson, under-secretary for humanitarian affairs, made his first visit to Sudan. He asked the government many questions about the allegations of ethnic cleansing and the forced relocation of Nuba to camps in North Kordofan. Before his visit to Sudan, Eliasson had been urged both by Africa Watch and NMSA to press for full access to all parts of the Nuba Mountains, including displaced camps.[25] NMSA urged him to "look for villages that used to be dotted around Kadugli, such as Kaiga Damek, Miri, Korongo Abdallah, Sabori, Lagori, Katcha and Torugi. They all have been destroyed by government armed forces and its allied Arab militia."[26] Eliasson did not go to the Nuba Mountains, as he was not planned to go to the region this time but he promised to send his Deputy, Charles le Meuniere. Le Meuniere visited Sudan on 20 November and went to the Nuba Mountains. But his report was never made public.

Faced with the huge volume of evidence presented to the UN, the commission on human rights in its forty-seventh session discussed the situation of human rights in Sudan. On 28 July 1992 the commission approved the appointment of Dr. Gaspar Biro as Special Rapporteur on human rights in Sudan.[27]

When he visited Sudan in December 1994, Dr. Biro noted that human rights violations were so extensive that they constituted a threat to the entire population. In his report he said hundreds of civilians, Moslems and Christians, who had been murdered by the army, the Popular Defence Forces and the militia in the course of attacks on Nuba villages suspected of collaborating with the SPLA. According to the testimony given.

Villages would first be surrounded and shelled in order to clear the area of any SPLA soldiers. After the shelling, ground troops would enter the area, shooting at random and often executing young men on the spot. Several sources suggested that the army and popular Defence Forces have carte blanche in these operations: anybody carrying a weapon, any young men trying to flee or resist arrest seems to be at risk of execution.

The state of Kordofan was reported to be one of the areas where the Jihad was not only part of government propaganda but also part of daily life in zones of armed conflict in the Nuba Mountains.

On 22 November 1993, Biro told the UN General Assembly of his great concern over the violations committed against the Nuba. He said:

The violations committed by the Sudanese army and the paramilitary forces under its control exceed by far the derogation permitted under a state of emergency and seem to be of such grave nature that the fate of the Nuba communities in the area may be questioned.[28]

On 30 January 1995, Dr. Biro drew attention to the horrific situation facing children displaced from the South and Nuba Mountains. He said that children working in the streets of Khartoum and other major cities in northern Sudan are rounded up and transported to special camps, the existence of which is not disclosed in many cases, and are subjected to religious conversion and ideological indoctrination. The Special Rapporteur was also alarmed by the large number of internally displaced persons and victims of discrimination in the Sudan, notably from the South and Nuba Mountains, including women, children and members of minorities who have been forcibly displaced in violation of their human rights and who are in need of relief, assistance and protection.[29]

Despite the bitter sufferings of the Nuba people, the international community has remained silent. The campaign on behalf of the Nuba people has been entirely non-governmental: it has been led by a small but committed group of Sudanese NGOs (notably NMSA and NRRDO), assisted by some international NGOs and human rights organisations. The successes of the campaign include opening up the Nuba

Mountains for humanitarian assistance, bringing the plight of the Nuba to world attention through the BBC and other media outlets, and finally bringing sufficient pressure to bear on the UN that it has pressured the Sudan Government to permit official UN missions to visit the non-government held areas of the Mountains.

Conclusion

The crisis in the Nuba Mountains is complex and multi-dimensional. There is the crisis of systematic human rights abuses. There is a humanitarian crisis, caused by war and poverty and exacerbated by the Sudan Government's blockade and use of food as a weapon of war. More fundamentally, the Nuba have suffered from political repression, economic exploitation and neglect and social marginalisation.

The Nuba have had high hopes that the world cares about their plight, and is ready to do something to alleviate their suffering and bring the human rights abuses to an end. The UN, the OAU, IGAD and the world's governments have disappointed the Nuba. But the efforts of committed individuals and NGOs have encouraged the Nuba to believe that the spirit of international solidarity in the face of genocide still exists.

1 See: African Rights, *Facing Genocide: The Nuba of Sudan*, 1995.
2 Sayyed H. Hurreiz & el-Fatih A. Abdel Gadir Salam, 1989: 'Ethnicity, conflict and national integration in the Sudan.'
3 African Rights, *op cit*.
4 Mohammed Suliman, Oct. 1992. 'Environmental Degradation: The Predicament of Displace People inside Sudan.'
5 Mohammed Suliman, *op cit*.
6 Mohammed Suliman: *Ecologist* 23.3 May-June 1993.
7 Suleiman Rahhal and Peter Moszynski, 5 March 1993: 'Sudan Government sets Nuba against Baggara', PANOS - Sudan.
8 NAFIR : Vol.1 No. 4, January 1996
9 Africa Watch, September 9, 1992. 'Sudan: Eradicating the Nuba.'
10 Human Rights Voice, November 1993: Volume 2, Issue 11
11 Sudan: The Ravages of War, September 29, 1993
12 Africa Watch, *op cit*.
13 African Rights, *op cit; and* 'A Desolate "Peace": Human rights in the Nuba Mountains,' August 1997.
14 Amnesty International, 29 September 1993. 'Sudan: The Ravages of War: Political Killings of Humanitarian Disaster.'
15 Africa Watch, *op cit*.
16 Sudan Democratic Gazette, October 1991
17 Africa Watch, September 9, 1992.
18 *Ibid*.
19 Amnesty International, *op cit*.
20 *Ibid*.
21 NAFIR, Vol. 1 Issue 1
22 Operation Lifeline Sudan: A Review, July 1996.
23 Operation Lifeline Sudan: A Review, July 1996
24 Africa Watch, 10th December 1991. *Op cit*.
25 Africa Watch, 9th September 1992. *Op cit*.
26 Nuba Mountains Solidarity Abroad. An open letter to H.E Jan Eliasson, UN Under-Secretary for Humanitarian Affairs, 11th September 1992
27 U. N. Economic and Social Council: E/1994/48, 1 February 1994: Commission on Human Rights Fiftieth session: Situation on Human Rights in the Sudan.
28 BC-U.N. Sudan. Gaspar Biro's Report to the U.N Router, November 22, 1993: Report Grave Human Rights Violations in Sudan.
29 Situation of human rights in Sudan: Report of the Special Rapporteur, Mr. Gaspar Biro, submitted in accordance with commission on Human Rights resolution 1994/79: E/Cn.4/ 1995/58, 30 January 1995.

6

The State of Sudan Today

Peter Woodward

The state of Sudan today is one which places the peoples of the Nuba Mountains in a particular position of conflict within a wider picture. Conflict has been taking place in Sudan for most of the years since independence, and has been both dynamic and complex. It is generally viewed as a primarily 'national' conflict, especially between governmental forces and those of opposition movements in Southern Sudan (Anyanya in the first civil war, the Sudan Peoples Liberation Army or SPLA in the second war). In this regard, the Nuba Mountains has often been seen as in a borderland between two sides. But conflict in Sudan has also long had local dimensions as well. A number of forces have divided into competing factions—not only the SPLA in 1991, but some of the units associated with governmental forces, as in Bahr al-Ghazal in 1998. Such conflicts within a wider conflict can reflect local and ethnic tensions. The experience of the Nuba is related to such developments, with military as well as social and economic pressures affecting the region contributing to conflict which links the local to the national situation. There are also international dimensions to conflict in Sudan. Neighboring states; regional actors from outside the immediate region; and superpower(s) have also been involved at different times and with different sides and groups. However this dimension has affected the Nuba Mountains only indirectly through the 'national' combatants rather than directly because of the region's geographical location at the centre of Sudan. Communities nearer to borders have often been affected by cross-border support for opposition movements and government attempts to counter them.

The Nuba Mountains' involvement in the complex experiences of conflict in Sudan raises the important question of why conflict has been so prevalent and stability so difficult to achieve. In my book *Sudan 1898-1989: The Unstable State*, published in 1990, I argued that the state was in danger of collapsing because it had failed to develop government institutions and a viable and peaceful political system in three main areas. The first was the rivalry between political parties which had been built around existing religious communities with a regional basis, which were incapable both of dominating electoral politics in Sudan and also of creating stable coalitions. Secondly Sudan's neo-colonial economic system had widened the gap between rich and poor, nationally and regionally. Much of Sudan's political rivalry was concerned with access to economic opportunity which was effectively controlled by the state. Finally the areas most discriminated by political and economical exclusion from the unstable and exploitative state were growing in regional and ethnic discontent. This applied not only to the South, but also to areas of the east and west including the Nuba Mountains. It had long been reflected in growing political assertiveness, as in the Nuba Mountains, as well as armed resistance in the South.

The coup of 1989 brought a new government which took a firmer grip on the state than any since Sudan's independence. It penetrated the state, purging areas such as the military, the bureaucracy and the judiciary. It reorganised the state introducing federalism, a no-party political system, and a Popular Defense Force to augment the armed forces. In its policies it reintroduced sharia; it sought to Arabise and Islamise society; it tried to win the war in the South; it repressed opposition in the North; it pursued economic liberalization; and sought an active Islamic international role.

The question by 1998 was whether in its nine years in power it had reversed the signs of a collapsing state. There have now been a number of partial or total collapses of states over the last decade or so, especially in Africa, and the symptoms are well known and can be examined in the Sudanese case. Clearly conflict continues in Sudan, and probably no government has effectively controlled less of Sudan's territory since independence. Signs of continuing repression of the northern opposition are still apparent, as the reports of the UN Special Rapporteur indicate. The gap between rich and poor has not been narrowed, and state services are in deep decay. The population's commitment to and identity with the political system appears weak, with not only violent opposition but millions leaving the country to live abroad. Sudan stands internationally isolated when recognition and support from abroad are needed to assist with its internal problems.

There are signs that the government is trying to change direction. The internal peace settlement concluded with some Southern factions in 1997 continues to be heralded as the solution to the conflict, including the recognition of the right of self-determination for the South. A new constitution has been written and a referendum held, although it contains ambiguities which only time may clarify. Peace talks have been opened with the SPLA, though progress has been limited. There have been consultations with the international Monetary Fund, and there are hopes of developing oil reserves. Moves have been made to improve relations internationally.

Yet it remains far from clear whether the crucial objective of peace can be attained. Will it be one side or other gaining victory in the civil war? Will it be by negotiated peace? Will it be a de facto division between areas under government control and those of the SPLA? Or will the present conflict, already over fifteen years old, continue? The answer to these questions remains far from clear, and in consequence the national context which is an important part of the situation of the Nuba continues to be extremely uncertain. Peace will need to come both nationally and locally before the sufferings of so many areas of Sudan can be ended.

7

Voices from the Nuba Mountains

The testimonies in this section are drawn from the work of the human rights monitors in the Nuba Mountains. The human rights monitoring programme was initiated in 1995 by African Rights and is currently administered by Justice Africa.

No1. A Victim of Abduction and Rape

Fawzia Jibreel was aged seventeen, from Otoro village south of Kauda in the eastern Nuba Mountains, when she spoke to African Rights the day after her return from three months in Mendi "peace camp." Her voice was very quiet and she held her head in her hands throughout. Her village was attacked at dawn on 31 January 1995. The names of the women and girls in this testimony have been changed to protect their identities. The interview was recorded on 11 May 1995.

Very early in the morning the soldiers came and surrounded the whole village. Our family has two compounds. They took sixteen people just from our family. The soldiers said, "You will come with us to Mendi. If you refuse, you will be killed." When we had been gathered, we had no alternative but to go with them, so we started to move with the soldiers. We were carrying bags of clothes-the soldiers took all the good clothes, leaving us just with the rags. They gathered us under a tree for the morning, with no food and water, while they were burning the houses. It took three-and-a-half or four hours. All the houses and most of the furniture were burned. They took cows and goats in large numbers, I don't know the total. They looted the best furniture and other possessions. By the end of the morning we were about 25 women and girls under that tree.

After finishing their operation at midday, the soldiers started making us walk to Mendi. I was made to carry a bed. The sixteen of us were all carrying things looted from people's houses, like big dishes, plates, cups and so on. On the way they said, "something you have never seen before-you will see it in Mendi."

When we arrived in Mendi, we were taken to the garrison. All the looted properties were put in one place. The people were then divided. The older women were taken to one place, adult women who had one or two women were taken to another place, and unmarried girls were taken to another place. Before we were divided up, the officer said to us, "Now you have reached here, every one of you will be married. If any one of you refuses, you will be killed." Then we were given a small amount of flour to cook and told, "When you are married you will have enough food to eat."

Five of the women were already "married." Three of them I already knew: Khaltuma, Nura and Zeinab. Two of them I didn't know. Those of us who were still "unmarried," the soldiers came in the morning and told us to work, carrying heavy things. Then they demanded sex. Those who refused to have sex were treated badly; they were forced to carry heavy things all day. In the evening, we were brought back to our place in the military camp to sleep.

After dark, the soldiers came and took the girls to their rooms and raped them. I was taken and raped but I refused to be "married" to any of them. The girls who were "married" were treated better. They stayed in the rooms of their "husbands." But when the soldier is transferred, the woman stays behind, whether she has a child or not. I saw some women who were remaining behind, but I don't know their names.

When you have been taken, the soldier who has taken you will do what he wants, then he will go out of the room, and you will stay, and another one will come. It continues like this. There is different behaviour. Some lady, if she is raped by four or five soldiers, she will cry from pain. Then, if the soldiers are good, they will leave her. But others will beat her to keep her quiet, and they will carry on.

Every day the raping continued. It continued during the daytime and at night. My sister Leila, aged thirteen, was raped. My father's second wife, Asia, was raped. They wanted to rape my Father's third wife, Naima, but she was heavily pregnant and she objected and in the end nothing happened to her. Another lady, Umjuma, who has six children, was also raped.

It is impossible to count the men who raped me. It was continuous.

Perhaps in a week I would have only one day of rest. Sometimes one man will take me for the whole night. Sometimes I will be raped by four or five men per day or night; they will just be changing one after the other.

We were made to work. There were different kinds of work. Some of us were made to go to the garrison to clean the compound, the rooms and the offices. Sometimes we were sent to Ngurtu, which is one-and-a-half hours away, to bring sorghum. When we are carrying sorghum, each lady will carry two tins. Older women with children were also made to work. Then, afterwards, they had to prepare food for their children. These women were taken to the peace camp, where they had to build their own houses. All the women, whether they have children or not, are given the same ration, of one cup of sorghum for breakfast and supper. So they worked for money or food. If there was no work available, they are forced to become prostitutes, so they can get something to feed to their children. Many women were forced to sell themselves for money.

No clothes were distributed to us. But any soldier can bring clothes and use them as a bribe or a payment for sex.

The only water in Mendi is from hand pumps that are just outside the garrison, about five or seven minutes walk away. The women go with guards to collect water. On the way, or when women are going outside to collect firewood, the guards are saying, "Why are you talking of going back to the Anyanya [i.e. SPLA]? Life here for you is comfortable. So don't refuse if one wants to marry you or sleep with you."

I did not see any people who had been in the peace camp for a long while. People are taken somewhere else after a while. But we heard that there are other peace camps where people stay for a long time.

Three men were taken from our village. One was carrying a bicycle on the way to Mendi. When we were inside, they were taken straight to the PDF for training. We never saw them again. Inside the town, men and women are completely separated.

There is a school, which teaches the Islamic religion only. All the Christians who are taken there become Moslems. There were some Christians with our group, and when we reached Mendi, they went to pray under a tree. The soldiers went and called them and said, "Don't repeat this. There can be no Christian prayers here. There are only Moslems here." But the Christian women objected and prayed again. The soldiers called again and gave them a threat, "If you pray again you will be killed." The Christians didn't pray after that, but they also did not go to the mosque.

There is a hospital, but it was not for us. There is no medicine if you become sick. I stayed there three-and-a-half months, but I never saw any pregnant woman. It is unusual.

Yesterday, at 5 p.m., I thought about escaping. I talked to my younger sister Leila, I told her, "Let us escape." My sister said, "How?" I said, "We will try. God will help." I told my sister, "Go to the hand pump as though you are going to bathe. After that, we will escape, because when you are bathing, you will not be monitored too much." I went ahead with the bucket. My sister was to follow. But she delayed, so I decided to go alone. I entered the bush there as though I was taking a bath, and escaped.

No 2. The war begins in the Nuba Mountains

The case of Clement Hamoda "Malidi", in his own words:

On 23 August [1985] the police in Kauda sent a warrant of arrest to [chief] Mohamed Rahma instructing him to arrest me. They offered to provide a force to accompany him. I have the document.

Mohamed Rahma and two men came to Tajura and arrested me on the next day, 24 August 1985. They took me to Kauda. In Kauda they said that your case will not be solved until you go to Heiban. They took me to Heiban and put me in the military barracks, not the police station. That is where I found [lieutenant] Maker Koriom. There was another man with him, Corporal Ali Kombo. Although his rank was only corporal, he was given full authority. Maker was a second lieutenant, but he was led by Ali Kombo because Ali Kombo is an Arab and Maker is a black person.

Ali Kombo said, "So they brought you." I kept quiet. Mohamed Rahma was there, and he asked him, "Is this the one you were searching for?" Mohamed Rahma said, "Yes, his name is Clement and Malidi." Then Ali said, "You are a rebel." I told him, "No I am not a rebel." He said, "We are sure you are a rebel. There are four things you must bring. If you don't bring them you will not see the sun. They are your pistol, your two-way radio, your two stars for second lieutenant, and your megaphone. These things you have, we want them." I said, "I don't have these things."

Then all the soldiers gathered round me. My elbows were tied behind my back. I was seated on a chair. When I said that I didn't have these things, someone beat me on the back of the neck until I lost consciousness and fell down. I was beaten several times. Then Maker told them to stop beating me until they did the investigation. So they took me from there to a big dormitory. Then at last they brought me for investigation. They told me, "You are from Tira."

I said, "yes."

They asked, "Where were you before?"

I said, "Khartoum."

"What brought you to the Nuba Mountains here?"

"I was born here and I came to see my parents."

"No. You are a rebel."

"I am not a rebel."

"You bring us those four things."

"I don't have those things."

"One of your colleagues, who was with you in school, he is now with us and told us these things."

I said, "Okay you bring that fellow to bring you the things."

Then I was beaten completely flat, almost to death. I was tied tightly, so the marks still remain, and two fingers still cannot function. I was tortured with a split cane, which was beaten down with a stick on the back of the neck. That was extremely painful. Another one took pliers. They took off my shirt and shoes. With the pliers they squeezed my penis. That man he tried to crush my penis; he caught it and twisted it. That was Ali Kombo. Maker was present, but Mohamed Rahma had left by then. From there, all my clothes, my body, was completely contaminated with blood.

When I didn't confess they told me, "Okay, you stay." And they put me in prison. I stayed and they brought one fellow, a Nuba, who fed me. I was still tied. When they took me for a bath, they untied me, but my hands and feet had swelled. I couldn't eat, I couldn't do anything properly. That man was working with security, they brought him to get information from me.

On the night of 24/25th I was tortured continually. After that I slept there while I was still tied, while the mosquitoes were feeding on me. So from there I heard them say, "Okay you may finish him." Ali Kombo said it. Maker was present.

At 6 p.m. on the evening of 26th I was about to be killed. So they tied me up. My hands were tied behind my back on two pieces of wood and my feet were tied to the wood with nylon rope. Each toe was tied up. At this point, I wanted to go to the toilet. The day I had been staying, when I was beaten, my whole body was completely exhausted and I could only defecate blood. Maker said, "Okay, take him to the toilet." He told one of those on duty to bring five soldiers. They were brought, with a lamp. When they came to take me, Maker said, "Increase the number to six." So there were six, each with a G3 rifle.

Then I prayed that I may be shot by these criminals, or I may escape, telling our Lord Jesus Christ that I should not be killed while I am tied up, either I will run or I will be shot. Then they came and untied my legs and hands. I pretended that I could not walk, as if my legs would not move. I still had the nylon rope on my toes. I said, "I can't go, I need that rope to be taken off." So they took it off. The toilet was a Sudanese style one. I was led by that squad of soldiers, three on each side, with one carrying the lamp. They accompanied me almost to the toilet. One opened the door and held up the lamp to show me. At that moment I beat him with my left hand, knocking the lamp into his face. From there I ran. When I ran, I ran boldly. It was 8 p.m. at night when the BBC was just coming with the news. I immediately faced another soldier who said, "Who are you?" I kept quiet. He held up his rifle. I rushed under it. Then he pulled back and said, "Stop or I shoot." Actually he didn't shoot. From there I ran I was completely helped by Our Lord Jesus. I stumbled over a thorn fence.

Then I heard a shout from the barracks, "Clement has run!" Three times. They shouted, "Where did he run?" Someone said, "To the market!" They ran to the market. I dodged them, running on the other side. I was hoping to run all the way back to Um Derdu to tell my parents to escape. From Heiban it is six hours to walk. But they had taken my shoes and my feet were very painful. I got lost and did not reach my village, I was in the forest.

I was afraid they would follow me by car. In fact they went to my village, Um Derdu, and they found all my family in the house. They took them to a village called Timbera, and from there they took many people to Heiban. They took my brothers and those who were Christians, and slaughtered them in

Heiban the same day. One was my oldest brother al Nur, another was a catechist from Timbera, Jimmu Ali.

The next day, Fadallah Osman "Mexico" was ordered by the army to take his truck and drive the troops to Clement Malidi's village. This is his story—which includes the first case of a church in the Nuba Mountains burned by the Sudan Government. (Ironically, the army officer who actually set fire to the church professes to be a Christian).

After the SPLA attack on Gardud el Redemi in July 1985, people thought that the SPLA was coming to the Nuba Mountains. At that time, Fadallah Burma Nasir was political supervisor for South Kordofan. He came to Heiban by helicopter accompanied by the Governor of Kordofan from el Obeid, Mustafa Mahmoud. He came and had a meeting with the army, and instructed them to deal with the SPLA in a military manner. At that time there were no SPLA forces in Heiban district. The instructions were aimed at those sympathising with the church: even if they were not cooperating with the SPLA, they may be anti-government agents in another way.

At that time I was a driver and a trader. The government was beginning to monitor the intellectuals of the area, including me, as I was a trader with a lorry and I went between Kadugli, el Obeid and Khartoum. When my lorry arrived in Heiban, it was always checked in to the garrison for a search, identification of the passengers, etc. From that time on the treatment was not as normal, due to the close monitoring. Nothing could be done without the police monitoring. Even Sunday schools were watched by the security.

This was the beginning of our problem with Maker Koriom. At first, the Mek [chief] of Kalkada, Mohamed Rahma Lesho, reported to the garrison that Clement Hamoda is a rebel. They sent a mission and captured him and brought him to Heiban. I was in Kadugli that day, 23 August. The next day at about 5 p.m. I came to Heiban. Clement was tortured badly, but that day he managed to escape.

After I entered Heiban they took the lorry to the garrison and checked it. Then I took it to my home. At 10 p.m. two security men came to me. One was Ali Kombo and the other was Abdala. They said, "We need the vehicle. We have an urgent mission." I said, "The truck has just arrived and it needs repairs." They refused to accept this and said they needed the vehicle straight away, saying: "If you don't give it you will be forced to account to the emergency laws." So I took the truck to the garrison.

When we reached the garrison we found some platoons of soldiers under the command of Maker. They said, "We are going to Kauda." We drove and reached Kauda where there was a police office. The police and security men got down from the vehicle and went to the police office. What they said there I do not know because I stayed in the lorry. Then they returned and said, "We go on to Kalkada."

When we reached Kalkada it was daybreak. We met Mohamed Rahma who said, "Let's go to the side of Tajura." When we reached Tajura, they were asking for Clement Hamoda. The people there said, "He's been arrested and taken to Heiban." The people didn't know we were coming from Heiban. It wasn't a military car and the people of the area did not often come to Heiban so they did not recognise us. When the people said this, the army began to deploy, going up the hill, ready for anything. I stayed with the lorry. After about fifteen minutes I left the car and followed them slowly. There was a church, Roman Catholic, made of wood and straw. That was the place where Clement used to go to pray. They entered the church. There was a small store with powdered milk and other things. Maker said: "That's the camp of the rebels."

Maker took matches from his pocket and burned the church. The other soldiers pulled grass and lit a fire to burn the store.

From there they returned to the car. Clement's brother, Ibrahim, had a flourmill there. They arrested him with five others. We took those people and proceeded to Um Derdu. In the riverbed of Um Derdu, between Um Derdu and Tajura, the car broke down. They left one squad of soldiers to guard the car and the captives, and the other soldiers went on to Um Derdu. I didn't follow, I was trying to repair the car. When some boys herding cows crossed nearby, the squad of soldiers said, "those are rebels" and arrested three of them. The other boys, when they saw their friends captured and beaten and crying, they ran away. The three were beaten thoroughly, tied up and put in the car.

After two hours, Maker and his troops returned, bringing five others. They were asking them, "Where is Clement? Where are the rebels?" All were tied and put into the car. But the car wouldn't move. It needed a spare part. I said to Maker, "There is no spare-we need to look for spares from Heiban." Maker sent five men to look for the spares. The whole day we spent in the riverbed. On the second day they returned with the spare part and we repaired the lorry and proceeded to Kauda.

In Kauda, the police said, "There is someone here called Daud who has a pistol." Maker sent a mission to capture him. They asked him, "Where is your pistol?" He denied having it and said, "If there is a case against me, say it openly." The Kauda traders came to Maker and tried to convince him that this man is working with the government, he is even bringing relief food (it was the time of the drought) and he has nothing to do with the rebels. Maker refused to listen. The man was taken to a farm. One of his relatives came following with his shoes to give to him, but this relative was taken and beaten up. He then left. Then all the citizens, even the traders, saw what was happening and went away. The traders shut up their shops, leaving the soldiers.

After breakfast we continued to Heiban. I put the people down in the garrison. There were thirteen prisoners, all men. After that the soldiers told me that I was welcome to go. I was given a warning: "Any time if we come and ask for the car, give it to us quickly. If you had not delayed us this time we would have found that man on the way."

When I went to my house, Ali Kombo of security came to me, and told me that if anyone comes and asks for information, don't give it, as this is a military matter. He said, "If anything happens, you will see." Then he left.
At 7 p.m. that day I began to hear the sound of screaming coming from the garrison. I was living close to the garrison and I could hear. I could hear the sounds of torturing and beating, with crying in the Tira language. At midnight, there was no more screaming. Then we heard the sound of rifles. It was a strange day in Heiban to hear crying in the night and then bullets. In the morning my father came and asked me, "Yesterday you went with the army, what happened?" I told my father nothing about who we brought and who they were.

In the evening someone who was a relative and a guard in the prison came. He said, "The people who came with you yesterday have been killed." I asked how he knew this. He said, "I was the one who went with the prisoners to dig a big grave. Then the bodies were brought and put in the grave and covered with earth." I asked him again, "Is it the prisoners who dug the grave or the army?" He said, "When the prisoners had finished, they left, then the army came with the bodies." I asked him again, "Have those been killed?" He replied, "All those have been killed." I asked, "Was Maker present?" My

relative said, "No he wasn't. The security guys were supervising the burying."
This is what happened, what I have seen and witnessed with my eyes.

No 3. The Survivor of an Extra-Judicial Execution

Mek Defan Arno Kepi is a chief, and the son of a famous chief, from Eri in the South Eastern Nuba Mountains.

In July 1988 many sheikhs and omdas [senior sheikhs] in the Nuba Mountains were called for a conference in Kadugli. When we were summoned, we were afraid. The SPLA had come among us, and we were hiding the SPLA in our area. The Governor, Abdel Rasoul el Nur, had warned us that he will deal with anyone who has SPLA in his area. We were already fed up with our treatment from the government-in that year they had already killed Sheikh Habil Ariya, Sheikh Adam Khidir and Sheikh Tamshir Umbashu, and two other sheikhs, I can't remember their names. Many others had been arrested. Two of our villages had already been burned: Kelpu was the first, destroyed by the Murahaliin, and Shawri the second, destroyed by the army.

We were 36 sheikhs and omdas who went, and one teacher. We were from all parts. Twelve were from Kadugli itself. We were seven from Otoro. Three were from Rashad and Delami, two from Shatt Safiya, two from Shatt Damam. There was only one Moro, as the Moro people were very suspicious [of the government]. Others were from Abri and other places. I also went with money to buy some goods for my shop while I was there. But we were all arrested and taken to prison. They took from me LS 46,000 and the clothes, blankets, watches and things I had bought for my shop.

I spent 59 days in prison. Colonel Ahmed Khamis was responsible for our interrogation there. Another one who was responsible is Sheikh Ismail Dana, he was sheikh of Debi but he became a government informer in Kadugli.

While we were in prison, some of us were taken out at night and killed. A group of seventeen was taken. Ours was the second group, numbering six. We were taken to a place near Katcha at about 11 p.m. by a group of soldiers. There were six of them, plus the driver.

We were tied with our hands behind us, and line up, with our backs to the soldiers. They were close, some ten metres away. Ahmed Khamis was supervising the procedure.

Then they shot us—ta-ta-ta-ta-ta-ta. Immediately, with automatic guns. I was hit here [in the back of the head] and the bullet exited here [through the jaw]. I fell on my face. My face was all blood. I fell but I didn't die. I knew that if I made any move, they will come and finish me off. I heard more shots as they were poking about, finishing off the others. While I heard this final shooting I pretended to be dead. The soldiers came and kicked me with their boots. They even stood on me with their boots. I held my breath and pretended to be dead. One said, "This one is not yet dead." The other said, "Let's leave him, he's dead." The first fellow was not convinced and shot at me with a pistol. It fell just in front of my face on the left side. The one who shot at me personally was corporal Ahmed Gideil.

They went back to their lorry. I heard the door shut and the engine start, and the sound of it driving away.

When the sound of the lorry died away, I got up, to a sitting position. Because I was tied with my hands behind my back, I cleaned the blood from my face by wiping my face on my knees. Then I looked around and found that all my colleagues were dead. Then I left. I walked for a long distance in the wilderness until I found a small hut, all on its own, in the fields.

I called out, "Salaam alekum." I said, "You people inside, come out and help me. Don't be afraid when you see me, I am a Nuba like you." A woman looked out. She was frightened and went back in and spoke to her husband. "There is someone outside who seems to have been knifed." When the man came out he was also frightened and about to run away. I told him, "Please don't run. I am a Nuba like you." He asked, "Which Nuba [tribe] are you?" I said, "I am a Nuba from Eri." He said, "Then why are you here?" I said, "I was brought by the army and shot." He said, "Are the shots we heard earlier this evening the ones you are talking about?" I said, "Yes." He said, "The army comes every night and shoots people in this place. The smell of the dead bodies is disturbing us and we cannot even stay here." I said to him, "I do not want anything from you except for you to come and untie my hands." Which he did.

I thanked the man and said, "As far as you have now freed my hands, now I will not die." Because the ropes were very tight and painful, the blood was not moving in my veins. The blood even burst one vein [higher up] on my left arm.

The farmer immediately took me to his sheikh. The sheikh said, "It is better that you stay with us here for ten days, and we look for medicine. Then we can take you back to your own people." But after four days, the sheikh came and said they had received a message from the army in Kadugli, saying that they had shot six but only found five bodies, and if the one who is alive is being kept hidden in your villages, we are coming to burn all the villages in your area. I told the sheikh, "I cannot be the cause of all your villages being burned and you being killed. Take me away. Throw me into a forest and I will see what will happen to me."

They took me that night to the bush. It was August and it was raining. I spent four days in the bush, eating only dust mixed with water. Some of this would go inside, down my throat, and some was spill outside, because my jaw was open [on account of the bullet wound]. After four days I reached Eri. I was already exhausted. I had no energy to walk all this way. Since we had been in prison we had been underfed-we were given just one piece of bread every day, and you eat one third for breakfast, one third for lunch and one third for supper, with only water.

I arrived in Eri and found my family. They did not recognise me. When I called my mother, she said, "Who is it? Who is calling me like that, in a strange voice?" By that time, the damage to my tongue and jaw had disturbed my speech. I said, "It is your son Defan."

My daughter recognised my voice. After they recognised me, they came to me crying. I said, "Don't cry, I am now with you."

Sheikh Defan's wound has healed, but he cannot eat solid food, and can only drink soup and other liquids. In 1999 he went for specialist treatment in Kampala, Uganda, so that surgeons could try to reconstruct part of his jaw.

No 4. Government Troops Burn a Mosque

The religious Fatwa of April 1992 directed government forces to treat Moslems in the SPLA-controlled areas as unbelievers and heretics. One consequence of this is the burning of mosques and the destruction of Moslem books when government troops go on operations. Churches are also wantonly destroyed-but the destruction of mosques is perhaps even more shocking, when it is carried out by a government that claims to represent Islam.

Imam Ismail Omer Damri is Imam of Kodi Ba Mosque in the SPLA-controlled areas of South Kordofan.

The government troops came from two sides at about 5.00 a.m. Some on this side, others on the other side, from Mendi garrison. Those on this side were burning houses. I ran and climbed those hills. I couldn't see them. Others were watching from the hills. The soldiers left the same morning, about 10.00 a.m., and then we came down from the hills.

When I came I saw everything was finished. The books, everything, was burned or taken. There were six prayer mats gone. Everything was black. Many books, 17, 18, 20 books were gone. They had written us a message and left it: "If you want to pray, come and pray in Mendi."

We decided to build another mosque. This new mosque was built after one month.

They say, they are Moslems. But at the same time, a Moslem cannot do this to a Moslem mosque. If they were real Moslems they could not burn the mosque which is the house of God and they could not burn the book which is sent from God.

Imam Ali Tutu Atrun, acting Chairman of the South Kordofan Islamic Council, was also in Kodi Ba when the village, including the mosque, was burned.

On that hill I could see everything in Kodi Ba very clearly. I took a good position and saw the Sudan Government forces moving towards the mosque in Kodi Ba market. They were running and spreading out across the whole village.

After they burned the area adjacent to the mosque I saw them moving towards the mosque itself. They entered the mosque with their boots on. They took some time and came out carrying books, chairs, a table and a carpet from the mosque. I saw six of them taking positions around the mosque's rakuba and library. The six soldiers pulled out matches from their bags and in minutes the mosque's rakuba and library were on fire. Then I heard a gunshot and saw fire at the top of the mosque. The mosque started burning from top to bottom. I couldn't believe my eyes.

I saw the government troops leaving Kodi Ba at about 10.30 that morning. It was a big force of over 300 men all in military uniform. At 12 noon I came down to check the destruction. We were fourteen persons. I found writings saying, "If you want to be Moslems, join Dar al Islam in Mendi." I found some books burned including two copies of the Holy Koran.

No 5. "The Eraser": Stories from an Offensive

The Sudan Government laid its plans for a 1997 dry season offensive in December 1996. At a meeting held at the headquarters of the 19th Brigade in Dilling on 29 December, the senior officers of the 18th and 19th Brigades determined on the plan of attack. Brigadier Mohamed Ismail Kakum was assigned overall command of the operation, code-named "Al Withb al Kubra" ("The Long Jump"). Brigadier Kakum is himself a Nuba, from Talodi in the southeastern part of the Nuba Mountains. In his career as a military officer he has served in various parts of Sudan and earned himself the nickname "Amsah" ("The Eraser"). It is said that he wipes clear or rubs out all that stands in his way. The conduct of the Sudan army during the 1997 Nuba Mountains offensive confirms the aptness of this name.

The main mobile forces for the offensive gathered on 25 February. A force of about 3600 men supplemented those already stationed in the front-line garrisons of Debi, Aggab, Um Sirdiba and Um Dorein. Approximately 120 members of the PDF reportedly deserted rather than fight.

"Softening Up"

In advance of the offensive, the army began its work on 20 February 1997. A military force including one tank and two jeeps with heavy machine guns came out of Debi garrison at 6.00 a.m. and moved eastwards. It set fire to the church of Nauli and burned the nearby village (150 huts). Many animals and other items were stolen but the residents fled to the hills and escaped. The following day the army in Debi reported to headquarters that it had completed a successful operation, attacking locations in East Debi, and that it had burned Ogo village and Nauli church and captured 51 civilians.

In preparation for the offensive, the front-line garrisons began burning and looting the immediate vicinity, while air strikes were called in to target the main villages where the attack was to be concentrated. On 23 February at 7.30 a.m., forces from Debi attacked Shwaya from several directions, burning and looting. The people of Shwaya were driven into caves and lost most of their food. The same day, further to the south, a larger force from Toroji garrison attacked the small town of Tabanya, using three tanks and four jeeps with heavy machine guns. They fought with SPLA forces, then entered Tabanya and burned it, but were driven back by SPLA forces. A total of 107 houses were destroyed, plus the church. The residents' food was destroyed or taken.

For three days starting on 24 February there was regular aerial bombardment of villages in Nagorban county, including Regifi, Um Dulu, Karkaraya, Achiron, Changaro and Kurcho. Although many bombs were dropped and a number of houses destroyed, the only human casualty was one man at Achiron whose leg was severed by a bomb blast.

Full-Scale Assault

The offensive proper began on 27 February 1997 with government forces moving out of their garrisons at Aggab, Debi and Um Dorein aiming to move into the most densely populated area under SPLA control. Three main armed convoys dispersed in different directions. One left Debi and moved to Eri, Tabari and Regifi. A second left Um Sirdiba for Karkaraya and Um Dulu. A third left Um Dorein and attacked round the southern flank of the Moro hills aiming for Dabker and Seraf Jamous. This was repulsed and driven back to Um Dorein, and later attacked and captured Dolebaya on the other side of Um Dorein.

At 8.00 a.m. on 27 February a large force moved out of Debi to attack Ndurba, Tandiri, Tabari and Regifi. It included two tanks, two jeeps with heavy machine guns and seven trucks, as well as a substantial number of foot soldiers. It first came to Eri, which had been burned twice before in the previous year, so that little remained. Thirty-two remaining huts were destroyed before the force moved on towards Ndurba. After fighting for three hours with the SPLA, the army entered Ndurba at midday and then burned the whole village.

The next morning, this force continued to Tandiri. First, two helicopter gun ships came and shelled and fired on targets in a wide area including Tandiri, Tabari, Regifi, Um Dulu and various places in between. The armed convoy then followed the route "combed" by the gun ships. After two hours of fighting with the SPLA, the army entered Tandiri. The soldiers burned 273 huts there, along with unthreshed heaps of sorghum and household items.

The force then proceeded to Tabari, which was undefended at that time as the SPLA forces were regrouping. Tabari had been burned a year before, on 23 March 1996 together with Tandiri. It was burned again on midday, 28 February. Among the buildings destroyed was the human rights centre. (Fortunately, the monitors were able to remove essential documents and equipment and, most importantly, evacuate themselves.) At 2 p.m. the army moved towards Regifi. After three hours of fighting with the SPLA they entered the town, and then they burned most of the houses, leaving only those they planned to occupy themselves.

Jibreel al Tahir Kuku was a resident of Regifi. A farmer in his forties, he is now living in the Achiron hills. He described the attack.

The army came from the side of Eri, up to Tabari. We didn't hear that they had come to Tabari, so we didn't know they were coming our way. We were expecting that they would be going to Karkar, where they were shelling and where the airstrip is.

We spent the night between Eri and Tabari at Ndorba. The next day the enemy came to Tandiri. In Tandiri they burned and then proceeded to Tabari and burned. When they came to Tabari the shelling was towards Regifi. When people saw that the shells were falling on Regifi, they ran. But we stayed close by, around the village.

At that time I was 500 metres away from the village. While the enemy was still in Tabari, two helicopters came to Regifi and began to shoot with their machine guns, and also fired rockets inside Regifi. While the helicopters were shooting and bombing the enemy forces were advancing. Some thirty minutes after the helicopters left the forces entered Regifi.

No one was injured by the helicopter gun ships because everyone had evacuated and the helicopters concentrated their fire inside the village.

When the army came it occupied the whole village. They destroyed everything. Any house properties were taken outside, and the houses were burned. In some cases they burned the houses with everything inside. Even the sorghum that was not threshed, they burned. Other sorghum was kept for feeding those who remained in Regifi.

Thomas al Mek Kuku is a former resident of Regifi, now displaced to the Limon mountains.

The army came on Friday. I was in the village that morning. I heard the sound of guns and ran to the riverbed. I stayed for some time in the bush, and then I heard the sound of a helicopter. At first I thought it was the noise of a car, but soon I realised it was a helicopter gunship. So I ran out of the riverbed to find a place with some trees to hide. Also three boys ran to the same place as me. The helicopter saw the three boys and began to fire, shooting three rockets at the place were we were hiding. The helicopter came close, and we just hid, lying down. It passed. Then it fired another four rockets in the area.

From that place I ran some way away. Then when it was clear I went back to the village. I saw the Anglican church was burning, it had been hit by a rocket. Another house belonging to an old woman had been hit and was burning, with all the sorghum inside it. I just stayed a few minutes, visiting my house, then I heard the sounds of cars coming. So I ran back to the riverbed. As soon as I reached there I heard them firing BM shells-eight of them-at the village. I ran from where I was to another riverbed further away. From there I heard the sounds of tanks and cars inside Regifi. There were some others hiding in that riverbed, they said there is no way out, the enemy has entered Regifi, and we must go further away, as they will fire shells and comb the area.

In the afternoon I was taking my family to a safer place, further away. We were going to Kwatang. Then the helicopter came for a second time. It dropped some shells but not close to us. When we saw the place where they had exploded, we found two cows injured. Around 5 or 6 p.m. we went back to near Regifi and we saw many houses burning. When I was running earlier I had hidden two tins of sorghum and a bag of clothes near the village. I wanted to go back and take more things from my house, but the machine guns were firing and we could not go close, so the only things I could take were those two tins and the bag of clothes.

There were two old women who could not run. They stayed. One, Kwachi, was burned inside her house. The other was blind. People saw her body on the thorn fence of her yard but what killed her is not known.

On 27 February at about midday, soldiers returning from Tabari to Debi found Halima Zubeir and others on the road and shot at them. They hid in the bush but were discovered. Several people were wounded including her daughter and sister. Bullets broke her right leg.

Coinciding exactly with the first armed movement out of Debi towards Eri, soldiers from Debi also attacked and destroyed the village of Ururi. They burned 235 houses and looted 75 sheep and goats. Whatever grain could be transported was taken back to Debi, whatever was left over was burned. A total of sixty people were abducted. The aim of this attack was apparently to prevent any SPLA surprise attacks on Debi while a large proportion of its troops were out on operation.

Also coinciding with the movement from Debi, forces moved out of Um Sirdiba garrison. At 10.00 a.m. on 27 February they reached Gardud el Himed. They burned fifty huts. In the afternoon they proceeded to attack on Karkaraya, arriving at dusk. There, they burned the village including three churches. In all they destroyed 325 huts and all the food except what they reserved for themselves. The people of Karkaraya escaped with very little.

Ishaq Ibrahim witnessed the attack. He is a farmer in his early thirties.

When the army came from Um Sirdiba, through Gardud Himed, and burned Gardud Himed, we could see the smoke. Our area has a hill and we could see for some distance. People came saying that Gardud Himed is burned. After that the army advanced to Libis. Any village they enter is burned straight away. After Libis they entered Karkaraya. Then they began to burn Karkaraya, and the smoke covered the whole area. They spent some days there and then advanced to Um Dulu.

Then all the people ran. Only a few remained with the SPLA soldiers. The army was shelling in front as they advanced. When they came into el Baro on the way to Um Dulu they had seven trucks. The SPLA withdrew to Um Dulu. We ran to the mountain, Tulumbi.

The army entered our village [el Baro] and overran the area. Some of the villagers managed to take some sorghum and possessions, but others didn't.

The force then moved on to Um Dulu, which it captured on 2 March. Sila Segendi el Tom is a resident of Um Dulu, who narrowly escaped capture.

By that time [28 February] I was in the village, still there. Some people ran before the army could enter. But the army was on both sides, in Karkaraya and also in Regifi. On Sunday morning we went to the church to pray. The army of Regifi came and entered Nyupum. Even then we didn't see them until they came to the village, and then they withdrew to el Baro. We were seven in the church, praying. When we heard the sound of guns, we knew the army had entered.

When we came out of the church, we saw the soldiers were close-200 metres away. When they saw us they fired at us. We ran. They carried on shooting but we managed to reach the riverbed on the side of Nugta. From there I ran until I came to a hill called Nabal, which is where my brother had fled with our families. By the time I reached there the army had burned sixteen houses. The church was not burned at that time. We could see them coming with two tanks, chasing one SPLA soldier called Thomas el Gere. They tried to crush him with the tank, but he did not fall under it and it ran over his hand only.

The same day the army went back to Regifi. The next day the army in Karkaraya launched an attack on Um Dulu. When they entered they began to burn the houses. By that time some people had taken their sorghum away but many people had not yet threshed so they could only take a little sorghum.

Scorched Earth

Having established garrisons in the heart of the SPLA-controlled territory, the government forces began a policy of scorched earth in the surrounding area. On 1 March, the forces came out of Regifi looking for cattle, and looted an estimated 800 livestock being watered along two riverbeds. The force used two tanks and two jeeps. The following day, a force from Karkaraya burned Labith village. 52 houses were destroyed and all the people displaced. On 3 March, soldiers in Regifi loaded four trucks with crops including sorghum, sesame, groundnuts, beans and other items and took them to Aggab. On 5 March, the troops from Karkaraya burned and looted Lupa village. The people were displaced and left without food. On 11 March, troops from Regifi moved to Tabari-Gambela and burned it after fighting with the SPLA. They abducted two women and returned to Regifi.

Thomas al Mek Kuku, a resident of Regifi, described the aftermath of the capture of his village.

The second day at the same time we went back close to the village. We saw the whole area was burned, except six houses, including mine. The soldiers were staying in these houses. I could see ten heaps of sorghum ready for threshing. Eight had been burned. Two were still there, next to the house with the soldiers inside. We could only look from a long distance. No one managed to go back to get anything.

After six days the problem of water for the animals we had taken became very hard. So many of the cows began to run back to Regifi themselves, to drink the water there. I don't know how many but many cows and some sheep and goats were captured by running back in that way.

The people of Regifi escaped with only their skins. All the food, all the possessions were inside the village and were taken by the army. In the outlying houses where the enemy is not staying, people who go back find that everything is burned. At most they will find only two or three or four malwas, enough for eating for one or two days.

Angelo Abu Sinena, from the eastern side of Tabari, is a farmer in his late twenties. He described how the army cleared the area around its new garrisons, looting hundreds of cattle in the process.

We were all in Tabari, staying with the animals in the riverbed, on the side towards Regifi. When it appeared that the army had entered Regifi, we ran with the animals. We went to Tilim village. I was with two others, but one, Hassan [Jelbora] was captured and taken by the army.

We stayed three days without going to any place. We watered the cattle at Koya. On the fourth day we returned to our previous place, to water the cows. While we were preparing the water, we were attacked by the enemy from Regifi.

They came with a tank and a jeep mounted with a 12.7 [mm. heavy machine gun] on one side and infantry on the other. On our side it was the foot soldiers. They took some 600 cattle, and we escaped with only a few. One boy was also there looking after some sheep; he was captured by the army and taken in a car. He spent fourteen days in Regifi and then he escaped.

The 600 cows belonged to many people. All these were taken. The few cattle that remain belong to people who succeeded in escaping with their animals. After the looting of the cows, some twenty youths went to the government side, chasing after their cattle. The army gave them back half of their cows but forced them to join the PDF.

Then we came to this side. First, we sent the cows up the mountain, and stayed in a place called Gambela, east of Tabari. After two days the army came to Gambela and attacked it at midday [on 5 March]. The village was burned completely. 67 houses were destroyed. The army shot the pigs and left them on the ground. They took the hens and a donkey. The people escaped.

Regular operations of looting, burning and abduction continued throughout March, April and May. On 27 March, the army came out for an operation to Tirum village and burned it without meeting any resistance. On the south side of the Moro hills, the Sudan army had not succeeded in establishing new outposts. But mobile forces based in Um Dorein continued to harass villagers. On 5 March, mobile forces burned Ramla village. 33 huts and all crops were destroyed. On 30 March, forces from Um Dorein attacked and burned Kurcho. They burned 21 huts and the church and abducted seven people (mostly women and children and including one old man).

Shelling

After the people of the captured villages had run to the nearby hills for safety, the army bombarded them with mortar shells and rockets. Jibreel al Tahir described the experience of the Regifi people.

The next day we ran to the mountains. Up to then we were hiding around the village, thinking that the army would go back. But when it appeared that they were staying we left for the mountains. Then [on 1 March] they began to shell the edge of the mountains.

A number of people were killed and wounded by the shelling of Limon and Achiron mountains. Asha Ukubey, from Karkaraya was killed. Five others were wounded in one place, all women and children. They included Samira Murkuz, Kaka, Keji Abbas, her small girl of one month, Jalila Kuku. One other was wounded separately: Ali Jibni.

From 1 March, the shelling continued every day. One mentally disturbed man, Kijana Kuku, was killed by the shelling. One woman was wounded. A boy from Um Dulu called Zarug Ibrahim died in a separate incident.

On 4 April, the forces based in Regifi were instructed to aim their bombardments at the top of the mountains, specifically Changaro, Lugi and Achiron church. On 17 April, in the shelling of the mountains using BM rockets and 120 mm mortars, two women, Asha al Tahir and Kaka Dixan, were killed and four others wounded.

Land Mines

After the capture of Regifi, Um Dulu and Karkaraya, the surrounding area was widely planted with land mines. Following the battles and the burning of villages, the people were scattered, hungry and without shelter. Their first need was to salvage what they could from their homes. Sila Segendi el Tom described how army operations made this hazardous:

When all the people ran to the mountains, they planned to go back at night and collect their things that remained. After the army discovered the people were coming, they found the path they were using, they came back and collected all the sorghum and took it to their garrison, and they planted mines on the path.
Ishaq Ibrahim from Um Dulu described the fate of one young woman:
Later when one woman returned to her house to gather mangoes nearby she was blown up by a mine. She died. Her name is Kwache and she was 22 years old with two children. She was brought to hospital the next day but she died. Two others were wounded [in that incident] but not badly.

Although taken to hospital, where she survived for 48 hours, Kwache had been too badly wounded, and the facilities at the hospital were too few for her life to be saved.

Nima Ahmed Madra, a thirty-year-old woman from Um Dulu and mother of three, was injured on 25 April, when she stepped on a mine on the road between Um Dulu and Nugta. She was still in hospital five weeks later, having had her leg amputated below the knee.

Tabitha Yoana, a 27-year-old woman from Um Dulu, was injured by a land mine on 2 May.

I was going to bring sorghum, at about 10 p.m. I was going at night because the enemy was in Regifi, and the enemy was also on that side. We went back to collect our things from Nugta, beyond Um Dulu. We made a nafir [work group] to collect these things, we went together to bring our sorghum from our house.
We went without any problem. When we came back we went another way.

In front of me were eight men. I was the ninth and some women were behind. The eight men passed then I put my foot on something like a stone and it exploded like fire.

Tabitha's right foot was blown off by the force of the blast. She was taken to hospital, arriving the following day, with the bone sticking out. Her leg was amputated below the knee, but four weeks later the wound remained infected (almost certainly because the damage to tissues continued above the point of amputation, meaning that she would require further amputation). The other leg was also injured. On her right hand she lost her thumb and right finger.

One woman following was injured by fragments from the mine on her face. At the time it looked serious, as her whole face was covered in blood, but she quickly made a good recovery.

Tabitha has two children aged six and ten. Having lost one leg she and her family now face acute hardship.

Abduction to Garrisons and Peace Camps

From the point at which new garrisons were established, one of the army's main aims is to depopulate the surrounding area and instead establish a captive population. Incidents of abduction are literally too commonplace to be able to list. A few examples will be given here.

People were at their most vulnerable in the immediate aftermath of the military operations. Sila Segendi el Tom reported:

After the army entered Karkaraya, a boy from there joined them. He said there are some people living in the bush, with no SPLA soldiers. So the army came and attacked them and took 33 people inside Karkaraya. Among them were my father and mother.

Surprise attacks on villages, in which large numbers of people were captured, were commonplace.

23 March, 6 a.m., PDF forces from Um Dorein attacked Nagorban, and burned all the houses and the church. They burned or looted all the food. The troops found most of the villagers present, and succeeded in abducting 190

people, mostly women, children and elderly people.

30 March, Forces from Regifi moved to Tabari riverbed at 6 a.m. and abducted ten people, mostly women and children.

17 April, 4 a.m., Forces came out from Karkaraya and surprised people watering their cattle in a nearby riverbed. They abducted 35 people, and also looted their cattle.

25 May, 12 p.m., the army of Regifi came on foot to the small village of Muro. They killed two men: Ibrahim Bidadi, aged thirty, and Abdala Gure, aged about fifty. A resident of Muro, Nasir Kumi, described the attack:

Ibrahim was killed while running away. Abdala was killed inside, he covered himself with a blanket and pulled the bed on top of him. Soldiers who were searching the house shot him.

Sixty-six people were abducted from this village. In total 130 were taken from several villages.

Earlier, troops intercepted some girls and beat them and demanded that they show them where the villages are. They stole some animals but didn't destroy the village as SPLA troops were nearby.

Killings

Some attempted abductions are targeted at prominent members of the community, such as educated people, administrators, Imams and church leaders, and chiefs. Those who resist or try to run away are shot down.

On 27 March, at Kululu near Buram, armed forces from Hamra murdered Kuwa Abdel Bari, the head of civil administration in the county and a trainee human rights monitor. Soldiers went to his farm at 7.45 a.m. and ordered him to surrender to them. Kuwa tried to run away and was shot. His brother Adam was nearby and managed to escape. Adam later returned to find his brother dead.

On 18 May, in what appears to have been a criminal act but is suspected to have political overtones, Imam Adam Kunda, a leading member of Islamic Council and teacher at Islamic school in el Eded, was murdered.

Other killings indicate the casual, indiscriminate way in which the Sudan army treats Sudanese citizens. Two incidents in the farms near Tira Limon, recounted by Sheikh Ali Jalboro, illustrate this.

On Saturday [30 May] the army of Mendi attacked near Karkar. They took cows and killed one boy Ali Lahma (eighteen years old) and wounded two. 232 cows and 118 sheet and goats were taken.

On Sunday [1 June] two people were killed. Ali al Birr was going to his farm. He was attacked on the way. They shot him and his leg broke, and then killed him off with a bayonet in the stomach so that his intestines spilled out. He was about 45 years old.

The second one was Jibreel Wolle. He was shot in both legs then they cut him with a bayonet on the neck. This was in his small hut at his farm on the same day. The soldiers from Regifi were responsible.

Also on that day, Osman al Tahir managed to escape. But he had to leave everything down there. There were people living down there [in the valley] but after the killings all the people have moved up here [to the mountains].

Aftermath: Hunger and Displacement

The suffering inflicted by the Sudan army in terms of killing and destruction is likely to be matched by the hunger that follows the forced displacement of people. The Debi-Tabari-Regifi-Um Dulu area is one of the most fertile in the Nuba Mountains: since the offensive it is deserted. Farmers who until recently produced enough food to feed their families and displaced people as well, are now on the verge of destitution. Herders are desperately looking for pastures for their animals.

Sheikh Ali Jalboro of Ndorba village, close to Um Dulu, described the material losses inflicted by the army.

We have been burned three times by the army. Then we rebuild each time and they burn again. We were burned twice in 1996 and once in 1997. From me they took nine cows, 25 sheep and goats, all the clothes for my children, ten sacks of sorghum and five of sesame. All the things in my house were taken or burned.

I am left with four sheep, six goats and fifteen cows. Before displacement the land was very good. It was large. Here in the mountains we have no good land. We have a small farm but we can hardly cultivate. It is the first time for us to cultivate in such a place so we can't be sure how much we can get but as you see the land is small and rocky. We tried to go down to the valley but we were attacked.

There is not enough grass in the hills for the animals. There are no places for them to feed. Up here all the land is farms. Even today we went to search for grass but we didn't get a good place.

The sheikh is a relatively fortunate man. Many of the others displaced to the mountains have no livestock to fall back upon. A group of displaced people explained:

Now we are borrowing, begging from our relatives. Those who have money can buy. Some people work for daily rates but it is hard to find someone who can hire you for work. Most people here are remaining only with their hands. They have nothing else to sell. There is no food in the market, not even if there is money to buy. Some people can eat the fruits of trees and bushes. But they are in short supply. People get by day by day. You eat what you have today and leave tomorrow for God.

At times like this, traditional knowledge about the edible properties of various wild plants becomes essential for survival. The hungry people rely on a variety of fruits and grasses, available at different times of year. But unfortunately the most nutritious and widely available fruits, such as the doleib palm, grow in the valleys close to army garrisons. Some people have been abducted while trying to gather doleib from the valleys.

A few people surrendered to the government, hoping for food rations. The government is actively soliciting support from humanitarian agencies for the internees in garrisons and peace camps, calling them "returnees" from the SPLA and announcing that it plans to provide them with "development". But hunger is also prevalent in the peace camps and people greatly value their freedom.

Postscript: Brigadier Mohamed Kakum, the "Eraser", drove over a landmine in February 2000 and was killed. The following day the Sudan air force attacked the village of Kauda, hitting a school and killing fourteen schoolchildren and one teacher, and injuring many more.

8

The Survival of the Nuba

David Stewart-Smith

Curiously, one of the reasons the Nuba became known to the world at large was a photograph taken in the late forties by the renowned British photographer George Rodger. It showed a triumphant wrestler raised up on the shoulders of a fellow competitor. That photograph brought the Nuba to the attention of the general public. Their culture, both then and now, is so rich and undiluted by the effects and influences either of western civilisation or Islamic fundamentalism that it is often hard to believe that such a culture can exist today. The Nuba's Africa is the Africa of old, not the Africa of coffee table books or romantic films.

Of all Nuba traditions, wrestling is the most acclaimed. Often entire villages will walk for many hours to watch or take part in a match. While the onlookers create a circle and watch in silence, the contestants, most of whom are soldiers with the SPLA, cover their bare bodies in white ash before they begin to wrestle. The contest usually lasts for two or three hours from late afternoon until dusk, when the sun is at its least vicious. Whoever topples his opponent to the ground first is the victor, and the wrestler who defeats all his opponents is the champion. There is no prize, but immense kudos for the winners, who are occasionally rewarded with an animal's tail as a symbol of their status. Any man wearing three tails is considered the greatest and most courageous of wrestlers.

The Nuba calendar is defined by festivals, or Sibar. Festivals can be spontaneous, just as wrestling matches can be, but they are generally part of tradition. The Harvest Festival (sometimes known as The Beer Festival) is the most important of all the gatherings, and it usually takes place in late November or early December, timed to coincide with a full moon. Its two vital features are beer (made from the staple crop, sorghum) and dance, and it is essentially a celebration of a good harvest. Obviously a rich harvest means greater security for the community as there is less chance of a food shortage (one of the Khartoum government's most effective weapons is the destruction of the sorghum crop). That aside, this festival is the best place for the young to meet. They wear their finest clothes, an often curious mix of African and Western styles, but some still arrive virtually nude, if it is their tribal tradition. The ultimate fashion of the day was fake Ray Ban sunglasses worn with a gentleman's umbrella.

As the people dance the Bokhsa, a few men stand in the middle blowing cattle horns. The women dance in a circular shuffling motion in one direction and the men do the same in the opposite direction, their arms raised about their heads. The noise, dust and smell are like no other on earth. An energy emanates from the people: the moon is full and rising over a crowd of over 2,000 people who have walked for perhaps eight hours to join the festival. The kujur holy men watch over the dancers and rain blessings all around. The dancing and festivities go on until late in the night.

Kujur also bless the cattle, to keep them safe from evil spirits and to give them strength (the Nuba, unlike the Dinka of Southern Sudan, do not drink the blood of their cattle). Mock stick fighting breaks out during the blessing to symbolise protection against theft and the holy men encourage the spectacle by throwing dust and ash. For cattle are the ultimate sign of wealth. A rotund stomach on a man is a sure sign of a person who owns a large herd. Few Nuba own more than half a dozen cows, but there are one or two cattle barons who own up to four hundred beasts. Another sign of wealth is nut oil.

Each tribe has its own traditions, and for the women of Shatt Safiya village a glossy covering of ground nut oil mixed with a rich red pigment is a sign of beauty. Women of all ages practice this art as it also indicates wealth. For other tribes, however, wealth may be denoted by a brightly coloured cotton dress bought from a local market.

I photographed a fifteen-year-old girl called Kaka Benjos, who was engaged to be married. She is the eldest daughter, and as tradition demands in her family, must be kept inside for five months prior to her marriage, not permitted to do anything. The purpose of this five-month ruling is to allow brides to become fat and so, during this period, they are fed the best food. Kaka Benjos was not allowed to wash, collect water, or prepare food. On the morning of her wedding, she was washed and then covered in a fine layer of ground nut oil. No one was allowed to see her except very close family and a few girl friends. As is custom, her future husband's friends attempted a playful break-in to steal her away. This pretence was carried out so that Kaka Benjos's dowry might not be paid (four cattle, one calf and three goats).

Eventually, after some of her parent's hut was destroyed during the mock fighting, Kaka was led out of the hut by her father into the centre of a gathering crowd. More oil was poured over her face and body before she was presented to her future husband. Together, they led the village on into the dancing and celebrations.

A tribal area may only consist of a small hill, surrounded by some flatter plains. Each of the fifty or so tribes have different languages. In one day's walk you may go through six different tribal areas, each with their own religion and customs. The universal language is Arabic. Some people wear western clothes, others are largely nude and wear the traditional loincloth, and each village has its own distinct style of hut building.

The acorn style hut with its rounded thatched roof and "keyhole" shaped doorway is designed so that the women can carry in wood and water without taking their load from their heads. There are sleeping benches on either side of the entrance hut, and you go through this before coming to a 6-meter square courtyard surrounded by further huts for storage, cooking, sleeping area, or occasional guests. At night a woven twig gate is pulled over the keyhole doorway, and an adult will sleep in the first hut for security.

It is man's work to build these houses, harvest the sorghum, plant crops and look after the cattle; the women prepare food, and carry the harvest and water back to the villages. There is no such thing as a cash crop in the Nuba Mountains. Nuba economy is largely based on barter, though there are markets where you can buy honey, salt and soap. Soap and salt are highly priced commodities, and because they are a rarity, have become a kind of currency in their own right.

Much has changed and little has changed since Rodger's photographs brought the Nuba culture to the world. The pride and courage of these people has meant that they have endured unimaginable hardship and cruelty rather than give in to outside forces. The Nuba have survived by themselves, through civil war, the coming of the missionary and the progression from spears to Kalashnikov weapons. Superficial change belies the ancient and enduring principles that lie beneath. Ask any Nuba what he or she wants; more often than not it is peace to do their own thing, to quietly carve their path into the modern world while retaining their cultural identity.

Photographs on following pages:

Photographs 1-14 reproduced with thanks to David Stewart-Smith. The photographs were taken in 1995.

1. Panoramic view of a Sibr.
2. Wrestling match at Shwaya village.
3. Wrestlers in action.
4. The wrestling champion is carried on the shoulder of his supporter.
5. On the way to a Sibr, two herdsmen fight playfully.
6. Child being painted with ash at the harvest festival at Shatt Damam.
7. Dancing the Bokhsha dance during the harvest festival at Shatt Damam village.
8. An SPLA soldier blows a horn at a Sibr festival.
9. Children play in jebels near Tamadirgo village.
10. Mother and child in front of a traditional acorn-shaped house near Tabuli village.
11. Mother and child walking to the village, Katcha.
12. Nuba man with a spear at Tamadirgo village
13. Nuba fighter armed with gun and knife
14. The feet of an SPLA fighter.

Others

15. Delegates to the Nuba Advisory Council vote
Suleiman Rahhal
16. Judicial Conference in session (left to right: Simon Noah, human rights monitor, later murdered by the Sudan army in 1998, Yoanes Ajawin of Justice Africa, Yousif Kuwa Mekki)
Daud Sadiq Karkon
17. Neroun Phillip Kuku, head of NRRDO
18. Victim of Sudan Government aerial bombing of Kauda School, 8 February 2000.
Yoanes Ajawin

Photographs B.1–14 reproduced with thanks to David Stewart Smith. The photographs were taken in 1995.

B.1. Panoramic view of a Sibr.

B.2. Wrestling match at Shwaya village.

B.3. Wrestlers in action.

B.4. The wrestling champion is carried on the shoulder of his supporter.

B.5. On the way to a Sibr, two herdsmen fight playfully.

B.6. Child being painted with ash at the harvest festival at Shatt Damam.

B.7. Dancing the Bokhsha dance during the harvest festival at Shatt Damam village.

B.8. An SPLA soldier blows a horn at a Sibr festival.

B.9. Children play in jebels near Tamadirgo village.

B.10. Mother and child in front of a traditional acorn-shaped house near Tabuli village.

B.11. Mother and child walking to the village, Katcha.

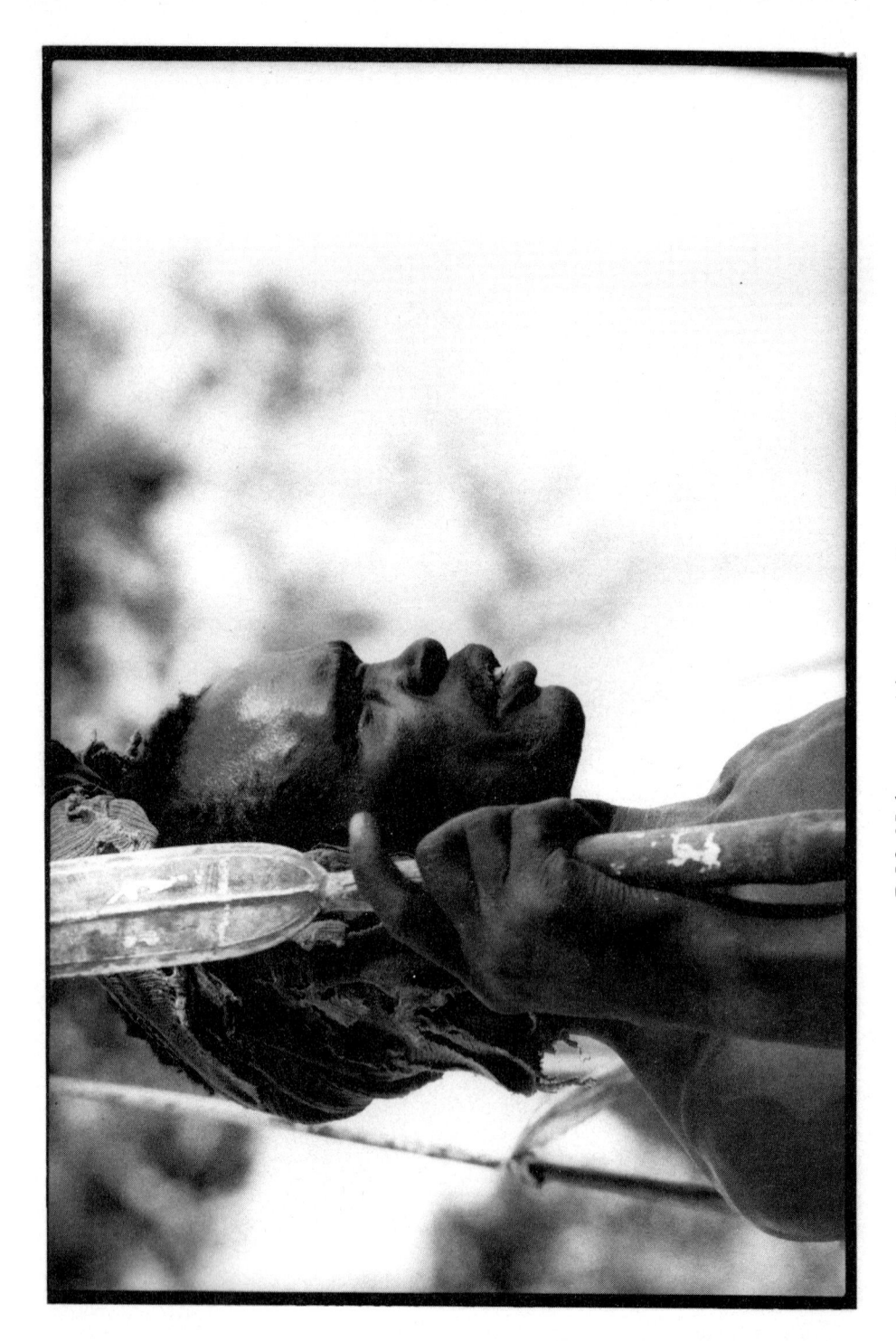

B.12. Nuba man with a spear at Tamadirgo village

B.13. Nuba fighter armed with gun and knife

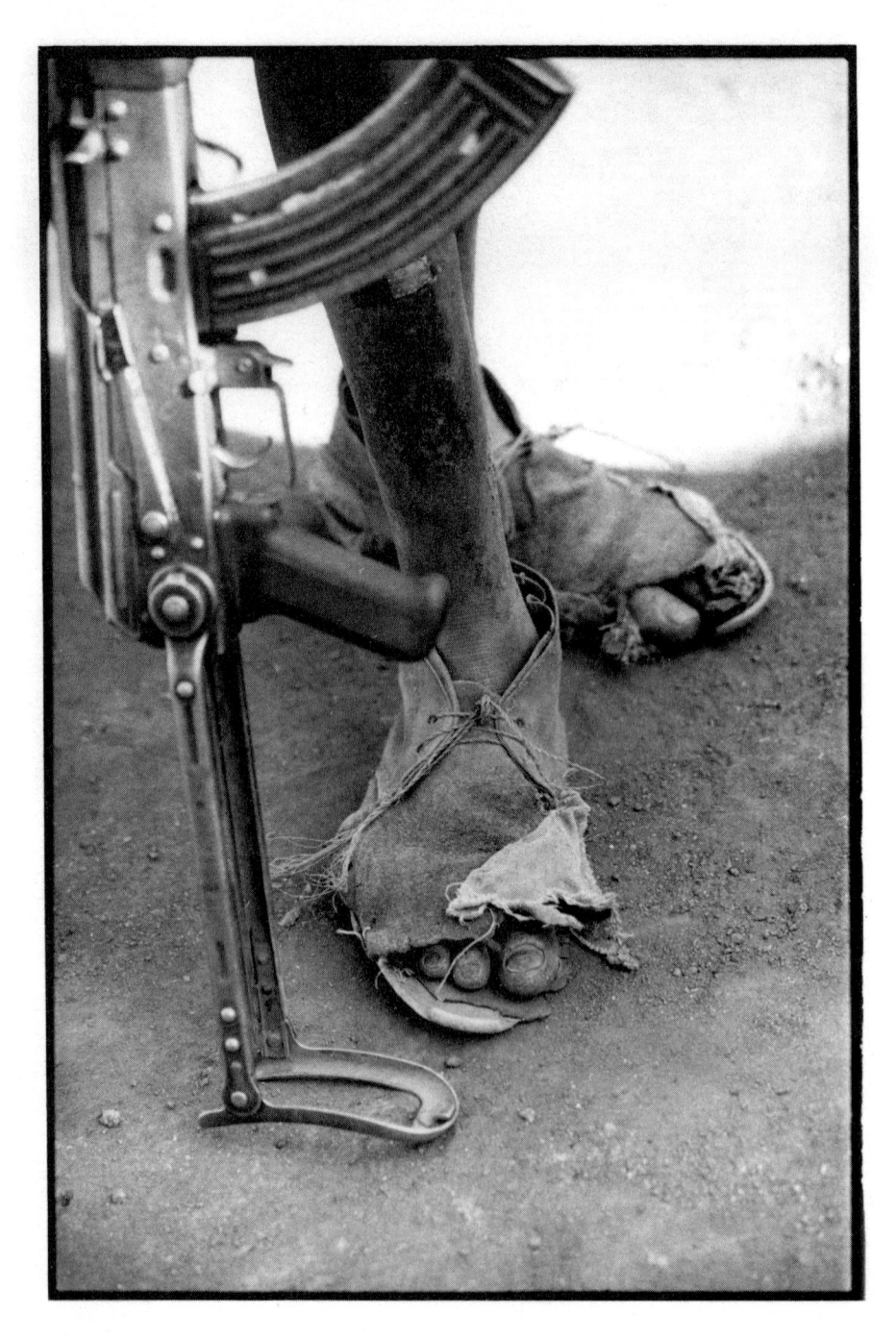

B.14. The feet of an SPLA fighter.

B.15. Delegates to the Nuba Advisory Council vote. *(Suleiman Rahhal, 1997)*

B.16. Judicial Conference in session (left to right: Simon Noah, human rights monitor, later murdered by the Sudan army in 1998, Yoanes Ajawin of Justice Africa, Yousif Kuwa Mekki)
(Daud Sadiq Karkon, 1995)

B.17. Neroun Phillip Kuku, head of NRRDO

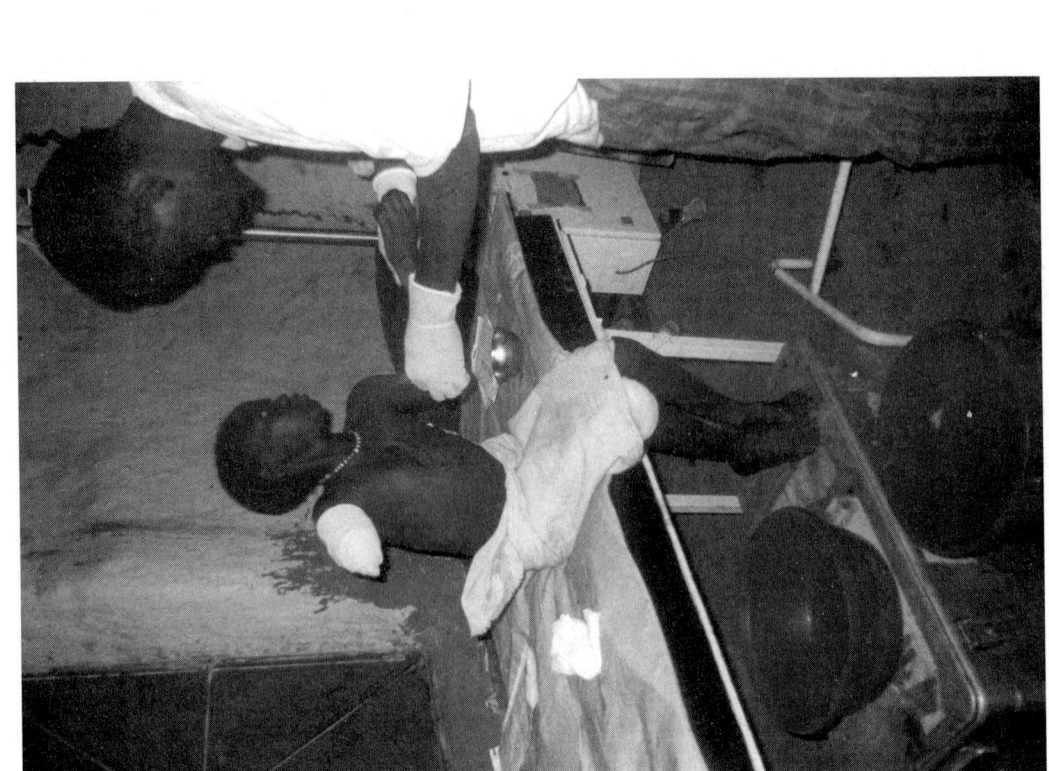

(left) B.18. Victim of Sudan Government aerial bombing of Kauda School, 8 February 2000. (*Yoanes Ajawin, 2000*)

9

The Nub Relief Rehabilitation and Development Organisation (NRRDO)

Neroun Phillip A. Kuku
Executive Director, NRRDO

Introduction

For most of the long years of war, the Nuba Mountains region has been cut off from the rest of the world due to the government's deliberate policies of blockade and using food as a weapon of war. These inhuman policies have forced many Nuba civilians to leave their villages and move to government-controlled areas in search of medicines, food, seeds and essential commodities such as clothes, soap and even water. Once on government-controlled land, however, they are trapped by the government and usually taken into "peace villages" where some are brutally abused and others are trained and sent to fight their own people.

The Government continuously refused international humanitarian agencies including Operation Lifeline Sudan access to the Nuba Mountains. It only began to relent, under massive international pressure, in 1999. Until then, the only humanitarian assistance provided was delivered "illegally", by Sudanese and international NGOs. The first and largest of these organisations, the Nub Relief Rehabilitation and Development Organisation (NRRDO)[1] was established in 1994 in solidarity with the Nuba people, whose overwhelming wish is to resist the annihilation of their culture and society and who to this end welcome international assistance that is given freely and impartially in conformity with human rights. At the moment, relief can only be given freely and impartially in the areas of the Nuba Mountains not controlled by the government and, outside the Mountains, to Nuba refugees in Southern Sudan and neighbouring countries such as Uganda and Kenya.

The Nuba population living in SPLA-controlled areas is estimated at just over half a million. For administration purposes the area has been divided into seven counties: Heiban, Nagorban, Dilling, Delami, Buram, Lagawa and Western Kadugli.

In the years since the war entered the Nuba Mountains in 1985, fundamental changes have taken place in the Nuba society. There has been massive displacement, food shortages and depopulation of the area. The Nuba's economic and social infrastructure, including health and education services, have virtually been destroyed. The fighting, looting and the burning of food stores and villages, and the loss of farming land and livestock, have created shortages in the basic necessities of the Nuba people who have become more and more vulnerable. They suffer from malnutrition, outbreaks of epidemic diseases due to the lack of medicine and health facilities. Many people have become either orphans, widows or disabled by the atrocities and reprisals of the government forces.

Humanitarian Embargo

From the outbreak of the war in 1985 until June 1999, the Sudan government maintained a strict policy of denying humanitarian access to the SPLA-held areas of the Nuba Mountains. The area was declared closed for all movement of food and basic commodities in order to seal off the region and force its inhabitants to flee SPLA-controlled areas. At various times, especially from 1990 to 1993 and again in 1997, the humanitarian and food embargo imposed upon the Nuba Mountains resulted in severe food shortages. The situation was exacerbated by the intensive raiding of villages and livestock that drove many Nuba from their fertile land. Famine and displacement were, and still are, used as weapons of war by the Sudan Government. Civilians were faced with a cruel choice: to remain in their villages and suffer constant attacks and food shortages, or to abandon their land.

On 21 June 1999, more than ten years after Operation Lifeline Sudan was launched, the first United Nations assessment mission ever visited the non-government held areas. This was followed by a second, more detailed assessment mission in September-October, which has raised the hopes of the Nuba people that at long last the UN may come to their assistance.

International Response

The mandate of the UN's Operation Lifeline Sudan (OLS) is to deliver aid to all war-affected areas of Sudan. At the time of writing, however, OLS has delivered no assistance of any kind to SPLA-held areas of the Nuba Mountains despite the humanitarian crisis - well-documented now in films such as the BBC's "Sudan's Secret war" and in books such as African Rights' "Facing Genocide - the Nuba of Sudan" published in 1995.

The OLS has been continually handcuffed by the issue of sovereignty even though the time of absolute sovereignty in Sudan has long since passed. Neither the Geneva Convention nor the International Convention on the Rights of the Child allow sovereignty to override the alleviation of intentional suffering. It was to protect these two humanitarian principles that the western allies intervened first in Iraq, delivering humanitarian aid to Iraqi Kurds in defiance of the Iraqi government. The same principle has later been upheld in various instances including Somalia, Bosnia and Kosovo. But it has not been applied to the Nuba.

The OLS is not only politically unable to deal with the humanitarian situation in the Nuba Mountains, but has also been reluctant to carry out its mandate. On some occasions it has manifested a degree of hostility to those who wanted to go to the Nuba Mountains to assist the suffering people. We can quote a reply of the OLS co-ordinator and UNICEF Chief of Operations, Mr. Philip O'Brien, to a request from NRRDO made in November 1994 that OLS support a needs assessment in the Nuba Mountains. Mr O'Brien wrote that

I regret to inform you that it will not be possible for OLS/UNICEF to support this assessment though we are very aware of the needs of the people living in the area. The OLS mandate does not allow us to work in the Nuba Mountains or to support Sudanese institutions wishing to do so.

Continually, year after year, the UN kowtowed to Khartoum's wishes and refused to send any teams to the Nuba Mountains. After the BBC/African Rights mission in 1995, a reliable air bridge was established and the NRRDO began regular deliveries of assistance. Some international NGOs assisted NRRDO, and some also began their own programmes (chiefly in the field of healthcare) in the Nuba Mountains. But, despite the continuing demonstration that it was physically possible to get access to the Nuba Mountains, and the repeated demonstration of serious humanitarian need, it was four years before the UN took any action.

Early in May 1998, after the personal intervention of UN Secretary General Kofi Annan, the Sudan government finally agreed to allow OLS team of assessment to go to the rebel-held Nuba Mountains. This was as a result of an intensive campaign set up NMSA and NRRDO alerting the international community to the unreported famine affecting the Nuba Mountains. The campaign highlighted the plight of more than 100,000 people facing dire food shortages as a result of drought, government attacks and the refusal of relief flights. The campaign called upon the international community to demand the following humanitarian measures:

1. An immediate cease-fire
2. Humanitarian assistance, including OLS assistance, to be allowed into the Nuba Mountains
3. Free movement of all civilians
4. Independent de-mining activities
5. Help in bringing about a just and lasting peace in Sudan.

After many delays imposed by the Sudan Government, the UN team finally flew to the Nuba Mountains more than one year after Khartoum made its commitment. How much longer will it take before any assistance is delivered? What new schemes and manipulations will the Sudan Government come up with to prevent the UN providing any real assistance?

But the Nuba have not relied on the UN and foreign governments. The Nuba have relied primarily on themselves. Second, an international NGO Nuba campaign has developed, which has provided essential relief aid, and has raised the issue of the Nuba Mountains-especially the demand for the basic right of humanitarian access-loudly and repeatedly, so that the Nuba can no longer be ignored.

The Role of NRRDO

NRRDO is an indigenous non-governmental organisation. It was established towards the end of 1993 to address the humanitarian situation in the non-government-held areas of the Nuba Mountains, and became operational in 1994. The organisation acts as an implementing and co-ordinating body, mandated to solicit and manage humanitarian assistance to the war-affected areas of the Nuba Mountains. NRRDO has a main regional base where the chief regional field officer and twelve senior sector co-ordinators are based. As well as a liaison office in Nairobi, NRRDO is represented in the local communities at county, payam, and village levels. It has been active in the fields of primary health care, primary education, woman and childcare, emergency relief, agriculture, veterinary and community development. Capacity building of local county groups is an integral part of all NRRDO programme activities.

NRRDO's prime objective is to represent the humanitarian rights and interests of the Nuba people. It is also set to promote and facilitate self-reliance through programmes and projects of relief, rehabilitation, and development. Its mission and visions are:

1. Advocating justice, peace and human rights.
2. Soliciting humanitarian aid and support.
3. Promoting and facilitating improved leadership and self-reliance.
4. Co-ordinating and managing technical and material assistance for relief, rehabilitation and development.

The core values of NRRDO are

drawn from its commitment to building and strengthening the development and self-reliance of the people of the Nuba Mountains who suffer from marginalisation, war and poverty.

1. Self-reliance: NRRDO seeks to enable the people to utilise locally available resources in order to fulfil their basic subsistence needs in self-reliant ways and to build social and economic patterns and structures which are productive, sustainable and independent.

2. Community-Based: NRRDO believes that effective co-operation is one of the keys to success in the credibility and sustainability of its mission. NRRDO seeks to promote co-operation among all peoples and agencies in the Nuba Mountains and to operate itself in co-operative ways at all levels, with communities, donors, partners, traditional and civil authorities and other NGOs and international organisations. NRRDO seeks to model co-operation as a principle within its own organisation, among departments and its staff.

3. Respect: NRRDO has respect for people of all groups, regardless of race, colour, tribe, sex, age or religion. NRRDO values the views, perspectives and significance of the many diverse peoples, cultures and beliefs in the region and seeks to promote the significance and uniqueness of each within the shared interests of all, with the hope of peace, justice and unity for all.

4. Tolerance: NRRDO recognises that social and religious conflicts generate and exaggerate the suffering and poverty of the people of the Nuba Mountains. NRRDO views diversity as one of the social treasures of the Nuba Mountains and therefore promotes and practices tolerance and acceptance of differences as part of the necessary and best way of life for peoples of this area.

5. Capacity-Building: NRRDO believes that people are the most important resource in the region and seeks to build their skills to face the many challenges of their lives and to take charge of themselves as well as their future and the destiny of their communities and society. NRRDO practices the principle of building skills in its programmes and projects for the people involved at community levels and in the development of its own staff.

6. Loyalty and Commitment: NRRDO knows that the people in the Nuba Mountains have been severely wounded by the on-going hostilities, poverty and isolation and that the people have a desperate human need for survival and health. NRRDO is committed to helping the people meet these challenges. Its members and staff have loyalty with and for the peoples of the Nuba Mountains. NRRDO will not betray the people or the principles of the NRRDO in carrying out its own works.

7. Credibility: NRRDO strives to

maintain its credibility and fulfil all the requirements of a legitimate and effective NGO to gain and maintain the trust and confidence of the people in the Nuba Mountains, civilian authorities, other NGOs and international organisations. It will adhere to high standards of operation including registration, office and operation facilities, structure, leadership, personnel, finances, management and reporting.

8. Accountability: NRRDO ensures its beneficiaries and partners that it plans to use all resources well. NRRDO is committed to accountability, evaluation and transparency for its projects and programmes. NRRDO is obliged by its commitments to the readiness of all departments, offices programmes and projects, to provide technical and financial reports and to hold itself and its staff responsible for failures and faults as well as successes and achievements.

9. Effectiveness, Efficiency, Evaluation: NRRDO is committed to striving for high levels of effectiveness in carrying out its programmes and meeting its goals and targets. Despite the difficulties and costs of operating in the Nuba Mountains, NRRDO is fully devoted to maintaining costs at reasonable levels, promoting efficiency of operations and administration, and ensuring usefulness and impact.

10. Professional and Technical Standards: NRRDO is committed to fulfilling the goals of the organisation according to its professional and technical standards. The standards apply at all levels both in the Liaison Office and in the field.

11. Sustainability: NRRDO is committed to building community-level programmes and projects that not only promote self-reliance but also ensure a chance of long-term success and sustainability within the context and conditions of the Nuba Mountains.

12. Teamwork: NRRDO believes that people working together in unity to achieve their goals are stronger and are more likely to be effective than those who work alone. Therefore, NRRDO strives to work as a team and in carrying out its duties as one body. NRRDO seeks to impart the value of teamwork to the communities, organisations and peoples with whom it works.

13. Political Development: NRRDO believes that political awareness and empowerment is a crucial element of community affairs and socio-economic development. Therefore, NRRDO adopts people-oriented, community-based approaches that help people in the Nuba Mountains to become politically active and organised in ways that will contribute to their self-reliance, development and a better future.

Programmes

With the help of small number of donors NRRDO has been able to provide limited services to the people in the SPLA controlled areas in the Nuba Mountains. Followings are the programmes that have been implemented:

Health: NRRDO supports 13 primary health care units, two primary health care centres and nursing college. NRRDO also collaborate with other medical organisation in leprosy control programme and evacuation of war wounded specially fracture and amputation cases.

NRRDO is also building a capacity to deal with women's health issues. This is a particularly serious problem, with very high levels of maternal mortality. NRRDO has participated in the SPLM-inaugarated campaign to ban female circumcision, which is a contributor to these problems. In addition, the very high incidence of rape perpetrated by government militia and troops has led to serious health problems among many women and girls in the area.

Education: Over the last few years, the state of schooling in the SPLA-controlled areas of the Nuba Mountains has continued to improve. Parents have put up many schools, usually built out of local materials in the areas where they have been relocated as a result of internal displacement due to attacks by the government forces. Thanks to the intervention of NRRDO, it has been possible to revive the education sector after nearly a decade of neglect. Future prospects are bright only if there is continued support from donors. Schools need even such basic learning materials as books and chalk which are not locally available and cannot be secured from government-controlled areas.

There are about 75 primary schools in the Nuba Mountains region with more than 30,000 pupils. Currently 63 schools are functional. About twelve were destroyed by Sudan Government forces during the dry-season offensive in 1997. This led to the forced adoption of several children. Others were separated from their parents and taken to the so-called "peace camps" which are nothing other than concentration camps and where children are subjected to forced Islamisation and Arabisation.

The education programmes also include teacher training, the supply of much-needed school materials and specifically focussed curriculum material development that takes into account the cultural and social values of the Nuba people. More than one hundred teachers have already been trained in the new methodology of teaching and in the use of new materials such as textbooks. In 1999 alone 55 teachers were in service and a further fifty are under going a two-month course in Kauda.

About twelve tonnes of school supplies have reached the area but this is meagre compared to the magnitude of the needs of many schools. At the beginning of the year, curriculum materials were developed in Nairobi, Kenya, by the NRRDO education consultant and his assistant. A number of learning charts and books were developed in Arabic and some local languages.

Agriculture: The Nuba have rich fertile land and the people depend on agriculture for most of their livelihood. They have been self-sufficient except in recent years as there has been a number of years with inadequate rainfall. Coupled with the destruction of villages and crops by the government forces, this has contributed to food deficits in 1990-93 and 1996-97. Agriculture support include:

1. Provision of tools and seeds
2. Training of extension workers in methods of seed multiplication and mixed farming.
3. Provision of ox-ploughs.

Veterinary Programme: NRRDO targets 150,000 cattle and other livestock in the area. 50,000 cattle are vaccinated on average each year on a cost-recovery basis. The programme also provides:

1. Veterinary medicine and drugs for various livestock diseases.
2. Annual training for community animal health workers.
3. Control of rinderpest in the area.

Capacity Building: NRRDO is small indigenous organisation which has small capacity to meet its challenges. It is succeeding, but always with difficulties. Capacity building is provided in:

1. Organisational and professional support mainly recruitment of advisors for programmes and joint financial management.
2. Management and administrative support and training of Nuba cadres and local communities participating in the operations.
3. Organisation development and team building to assist improve performance.

Community Development: The programme endeavours to ensure self-reliance through self- help and income generation projects. The objective is to create linkages between and among the components of the programme which include:

1. Soap making and oil processing
2. Weaving and spinning
3. Blacksmith and carpentry
4. Co-operative farming
5. Neem tree development
6. Culture support and indigenous technology
7. Women tailoring and knitting

Access Development: The programme aims to cut the high transportation cost to the Nuba Mountains which is accessible only by air for the time being, with the long-term aim of opening routes by land to the programme area.

1. Rehabilitation of three trucks for road access.
2. Access basis at borders in Kenya and Uganda.
3. Cleaning and maintaining airstrips and bases in the Nuba Mountains.

Water Development: The availability of clean water supplies are decreasing as the war continues. The existing drinking sources of water are from streams in the hills, open ponds and surface sources in the plains. The programme aims to improve water sources by:

1. Provision of spare parts to the already existing 46 bore holes, which are mostly in bad condition.
2. Provision of hand powered augers for drilling boreholes manually to a level of 10 to 15 metres.
3. Community dams which allows for sufficient catchment of water using local material for irrigation of vegetables in dry seasons.

Communication: The lack of information on Nuba Mountains has seriously hampered efforts to respond to the crisis. NRRDO tries to maintain links with the outside world and create networks within Nuba Mountains. It currently supports:

1. Two-way radio network: Kenya-Nuba Mountains
2. Newsletter for Nuba Mountains (NAFIR), produced jointly with NMSA.
3. Radio programmes and a satellite link are required to improve communications.

Human Rights: To provide international awareness of the human rights situation in the Nuba Mountains and to awareness among the Nuba of their rights under international law. NRRDO is supported by Justice Africa (formerly African Rights) on:

1. Human rights monitoring and reporting of abuses in the area.
2. Human rights education by distribution of human rights literature.
3. Training on women's rights.
4. Support to the judiciary by training paralegal meks and Sheikhs in basic legal principles and materials support.
5. Inter communal conflict resolution.
6. Publicity, lobbying and advocacy.
7. Campaigning for the right of humanitarian access-supported by NMSA, INCC and a growing band of international NGOs and campaigning groups.

Relief Commodities (non-food): Because the Nuba area has been cut off from the outside world, there is a great need for the provision of basic necessities, including non-food items. Clothing, soap, salt and household utensils are items which NRRDO endeavours to provide on regular basis, especially in emergencies.

Conclusion

Given the nature of the Khartoum government's hostility towards access and assistance to the Nuba Mountains and the fact that the war in this area has been particularly brutal, all programmes are carried out with extreme discretion. Confidentiality in all NRRDO activities is essential and must be strictly adhered to by all NRRDO partners.

The entire assistance programme in the SPLM-administered areas of the Nuba Mountains is a triumph for NGO action. There have been no official programmes to assist the Nuba or to publicise their plight. From the start, opening up humanitarian access was the work of NGOs (NRRDO and African Rights). All assistance, capacity building, lobby and advocacy has been the work of NGOs—NRRDO, INCC and NMSA supported by a growing band of sympathetic international organisations. Finally, in 1999, the international campaign on behalf of the Nuba, together with the shaming example of a successful ongoing assistance programme, forced the UN to act.

It is obvious that the people of the Nuba Mountains have suffered especially in the current war and are far more marginalised than before. There have been grave violations of international humanitarian law and human rights, among them intimidation and torture, summary execution and violence against women, the elderly and the children with the aim of destroying the ethnic identity of the Nuba. These have been documented by various human rights organisations. For ten years the Sudan government persistently refused, within the tripartite agreement, to authorise the extension of OLS operations to the war-affected areas of the Nuba Mountains-and there are no guarantees that it will not try to block or manipulate the UN programmes that it has finally and reluctantly allowed to proceed. NRRDO, the sole non-governmental humanitarian organisation operational in the liberated Nuba Mountains urgently appeals to the international community to come to the rescue of the displaced, hungry and sick people of the Nuba Mountains.

---

[1] NRRDO was originally known as the Nub Relief, Rehabilitation and Development Society, NRRDS.

10

Nuba Agriculture: Poverty or Plenty?

Ian Mackie

The future of agriculture in the Nuba Mountains, like everything else in the Sudan, will depend on the end of hostilities and decisions taken by politicians. Productive agriculture sustainable in the long term will come only when the Nuba rights to their ancestral homelands are assured. By this I mean not only the rugged mountains and valleys, but also areas of the fertile plains that surround them.

It is many years since I first got to know the Nuba Mountains, and today it saddens me that land always recognised as Nuba land is now taken over for purposes of large scale mechanised agriculture by government policy: a policy where the only role, if any, for the Nuba, is as poorly paid labour. This basic issue, the fundamental rights of the Nuba to their lands, is one which must be taken up and examined by international arbiters, so that the present cruel injustice may be revealed to the world and rectified.

I address the theme of Nuba Agriculture: Poverty or Plenty, with the expectation that better times lie ahead, so that positive and sustainable husbandries may be established for the good of the indigenous people, the environment, and indeed the entire country. I know the land in question very well, albeit there is a gap of years since I was there! In my early trekking days I was given the task of examining and mapping this land, to discover its development potential. Since then my work has involved land use and systems of production. Incidentally, I was also a witness to the progressive encroachment of the outside tribes (such as the Baggara), an invasion that has reached its ultimate in recent years with dispossession of the Nuba themselves.

There was a saying in the old days that "the Sudan can become the breadbasket of Africa". The origin of this saying was the knowledge of the great areas of virgin rain-land such as in the Nuba Mountains. As I trekked the region I had a golden opportunity to witness the way the Nuba lived in harmony with their environment. They grew cotton, sorghum and sesame. Sometimes on terraced hillsides. Even on the rough mountaintops there were vegetable plots. In surrounding territory, other peoples used destructive "slash and burn" methods.

Experiments in cultivation methods (which I was involved in) on the virgin lands of the Nuba pointed the way for the best use of this land.

I have experienced plantation-type agriculture in the Gezira and was able to draw a conclusion which later experience has constantly reinforced: namely, that there is only one way of opening up virgin Nuba land in a durable and self-sustainable way and that is by using the work and efforts of individual farmers, on land they can call their own. Furthermore, with my remit to study soil erosion at that time, I witnessed the wide areas of eroded land and I became certain (like most people today who know this region of Africa) that the land has to be treated with care and sensitivity; something that does not happen when heavy machinery carves up great estates, as with the present government's policy.

In fragile Africa, machinery, which answers important needs in Europe and the USA, has less application and can be highly destructive as well as unprofitable in the long term.

The following points have shaped my views with regard to Nuba and the use of machinery on large scale.

1. From a husbandry viewpoint, huge machinery-pulled ploughs threaten the soil mass, which in turn is subjected to violent rainstorms, followed by months of unmitigated drought and wind. The organic value of the soil is lessened and in time it loses its fertility. In this remote African setting, with mechanisation, soil tends to treated as a medium to be exploited, rather than husbanded for years to come.

2. From an economic viewpoint, mechanised agriculture has a high cost per unit of output (particularly when high maintenance costs are considered). It becomes "extensive" (not intensive) agriculture, namely, large area-low yield. There are relatively few operations that machines can do, and inevitably output

depends on labour in the long term. This type of agriculture produces short-term gains, which progressively diminish. It attracts the kind of investor who expects quick returns for his money, but who has no time for the long view. It represents only an interest in profits, and not in the land or the people. Unfortunately, it can attract financial support from outsiders who have little knowledge of African conditions and probably judge on their experience of softer European agriculture.

3. From a social (and moral) point of view, it can best be described as exploitative. It is enough to say that the landlord/manager system, on large plantations has only too often stained history by its cruelty, and very often, slavery. It is difficult to imagine any justice at all for the Nuba in this system, on what is really their own land.

Mechanised farming schemes have a bad track record in the Sudan, most have failed today.

The Alternative Way

There is another way to open up Nuba land as I previously indicated, one that is durable and also productive. It carries with it the potential to fill that African bread-basket, and increase the country's wealth: namely by encouraging the Nuba to farm their own land according to a well thought-out policy; agreed by all parties.

I am not speaking of random farming by miscellaneous groups, but rather a unified strategy of developing new land with self-sustaining communities - on the grand scale. It is long-term: initially, perhaps, it is more difficult, but it is the intelligent way and is "just" to the people most involved. Let me explain my reasons for advocating this form of agriculture. At the end of the 1939-45 war, the Sudan government was faced with two major problems:

1. Thousands of returning Nuba soldiers needed new land on which to settle.
2. Soil erosion was shifting whole communities from their homelands. Both of these groups required the interest and the care of government.

In brief, I was asked to establish a village-farming community on virgin forest land, then to assemble all data of costs, production, social factors, in fact every item of interest, to find out if this was a valid answer to the two problems. All the data from this work is still available.

With minimal financial help and provision of new basic resources, the new cultivators set about building their own village (which became a model of its type). They started working they're allotted holdings, the whole family taking part, and at the end of the season produced handsome crops, with a surplus which quickly attracted trade. A communal hut was built and the village people settled comfortably into their new community.

Instead of the heavy fist of government, it was the gentle touch, which worked, and nearly always works when there is fair government.

Some technicalities are:

1. The government dug the "well" (or *Bair*), and gave basic support items of materials, medical service etc.
2. Small grants and long-term loans (for seed, tools, livestock etc.) were given to get the work under way,
3. The cultivators were left to run their own affairs and elect their own leaders,
4. Advice was always at hand to make sure optimum output was achieved.

There were snags of course, but nothing that could not be resolved. This, as I visualise it, is the right future for Nuba Agriculture. It was right years ago and is equally valid today.

Poverty or Plenty?

I have outlined, as I see it, after my years of experience, opposing agricultural strategies. One of these can only perpetuate the current poverty; the other one is worthy of deep consideration by every interested party. This alternative could, in time, yield the plenty that will transform the Nuba Mountains and the Sudan.

Finally, I believed a well-conceived plan of Nuba settlement on the good land of the Nuba Mountains can attract financial support from inside and outside the country when the hoped-for time arrives, because it involves the essential prerogative of justice, as well as the likelihood of economic success.

11

Democracy in a War Zone: The Nuba Parliament

Julie Flint

The South Kordofan Advisory Council, also known as the Nuba Parliament, was first convened in September 1992, at perhaps the darkest moment for the Nuba people. At that time, the very survival of the Nuba appeared to be in doubt, as they faced an unprecedented military onslaught by the Sudan Government, in the name of jihad, combined with massive forced relocation of the civilian population away from the mountains, and intense famine.

In 1991, the SPLA held the edge over the Sudan army. But when the SPLA split cut off the supply of arms, the Sudan Government decided to deal with the insurrection in the Nuba Mountains once and for all. In January 1992 it declared a Jihad and assembled the largest force ever mobilised in the entire war to that date-some 40,000 troops backed by aircraft and heavy artillery-and decided to re-conquer the mountains, hill by hill.

Their first target was Jebel Tullishi. Meanwhile the government embarked upon a policy of systematically burning villages and forcibly relocating the civilian population to camps in North Kordofan.

Commander Yousif Kuwa's forces were reduced to eating a single cup of grain a day as rations, and fighting with whatever ammunition they could take from the government army. Never had the future of the rebellion seemed darker. And, given the near-genocidal policies followed by the government, never had the future of the Nuba people seemed more in doubt.

But the Nuba fighters withstood the attack on Jebel Tullishi. A mere 970 SPLA troops under Alternate Commander Mohamed Juma Nayel withstood day-and-night attacks and bombardment for nearly four months, outnumbered thirty-to-one. But this extraordinary resistance only bought time. In 1992, Kuwa made two attempts to bring ammunition from Bahr el Ghazal to shore up his troops and stem a haemorrhage of civilians to the government side. Both ended in disaster. The first attempt was in the dry season, but 240 of the 400 Nuba soldiers sent on the expedition died after failing to find water on the only route left open by the intra-SPLA fighting. The second attempt was in July, in the rainy season, but three days of rain and flooding took the lives of more than 100 soldiers. It was, as well as a military setback, a personal tragedy. Yousif Kuwa explained, "The worst part of it is that they were very brave people. In normal circumstances, I would have resigned over that."

The First Advisory Council

Instead Yousif Kuwa asked for a vote of confidence from ordinary Nuba. A council was to be chosen by the senior members of the civil administration that was being established. And so the first Advisory Council met in Debi, a village in the southeastern mountains, in September 1992. It was a direct response to the greatest tragedy of the war so far and a first attempt to give the Nuba people a say in decisions affecting not only their future-but their very survival.

After four days of unfettered debate, the 200 delegates, most of them civilians, voted overwhelmingly to continue the war. "The past is my responsibility," Kuwa told the council, "But from here it is the responsibility of all of us."

Since then the Advisory Council has met most years. It did not meet in 1996, when Commander Kuwa was travelling abroad and requested a postponement, or in 1998, when elections were held to a new Council. (A smaller advisory group did however meet.) In 1997, the location chosen for the Advisory Council was Kauda, in the eastern mountains.

The 1997 Advisory Council

The 1997 Council meeting was the first that was expanded to include Nuba living outside Sudan. Commander Kuwa invited Nuba from the Middle East and Europe to travel secretly to join the debate, and then to rally support among Nuba abroad. But word of the preparations for the enlarged council reached the government, through their informers, and Khartoum went to great lengths to prevent the meeting from taking place.

Timing their attack to coincide with the scheduled opening of the council on Saturday 1st November, Antonov bombers based in El Obeid launched the most intensive aerial bombardment yet seen in the Nuba Mountains. Starting at dawn, bombers launched the first of four sorties that day on Kauda and the nearby airstrip. Five more raids followed on the two next days. It was a rate of bombing rarely seen in the war and an indication of the importance accorded to the Nuba assembly. The planes dropped not only conventional bombs, but also hundreds of cluster bombs. Luck, however, was on the side of the Nuba and there was only one casualty-the director of the Kauda primary school, 32 year old Farouk Moses Arad, who was hit in the neck by a piece of shrapnel while getting the hundreds of children in his care to safety. He was only slightly wounded.

There are no military targets in Kauda. The nearest SPLA base is approximately two hours walk away.

The Advisory Council was unaffected by the bombing. Unknown to the government of Sudan, the meeting had been postponed to 10 November because of visa problems encountered by the Nuba delegates coming through east Africa. And the venue was also changed to Gidel, in the mountains to the east of Kauda.

There is no doubt that the government's attack was designed to prevent the news of the Council-and the democratic process underpinning it and the vibrancy of life in rebel-held areas- reaching the outside world. The government knew that invitations had been extended to Nuba living abroad. Their names were broadcast and they were denounced on Omdurman radio.

The 1997 Advisory Council was attended by 308 delegates, three Nuba expatriates and six foreigners including three journalists. The Council was headed by Acting Chairman Musa Abdel Bagi Fadel, the Chief Medical Officer in the mountains, who was presiding for the third time. At least two thirds of the members of the assembly were civilians, selected in 1992. The remainder were appointed by Kuwa himself. Each of the seven counties administered by the SPLM send 25 delegates plus a number of "guests". The Christian and Moslem faiths sent seven representatives each. The SPLA delegation included a range of commanders.

Despite the difficulty of communicating in the Nuba Mountains, invitations were issued to every council member, either in writing or by radio. All members travelled by foot (no other mode of transport is available). Those from the western mountains had to walk for up to two weeks to attend, crossing stretches of no-man's-land where there is serious danger of army ambushes.

The Advisory Council itself was held in the open air, under a large tree, with the Executive Committee of the assembly sitting on a raised, shaded podium. The partial opening of the mountains under the aid programme supervised by NRRDO was immediately apparent in the organisation of the council. For the first time ever, speakers had the benefit of a microphone, and the deliberations of the council were recorded both on camera and tape recorder. These technical advances caused surprise and delight among the delegates. "We really see the Movement is going ahead. Truly we are a government now!"

The Executive Committee drew up a six-point agenda:
1. Evaluation of the SPLM administration and the political experience in the Nuba Mountains (including humanitarian relief).
2. Strategic future policy for the SPLM in the Nuba Mountains and ways of confronting the policy of the Government of Sudan.
3. Recommendations of the Executive Committee.
4. Presentations by Nuba from abroad.
5. Other business.
6. Address given by Governor Yousif Kuwa Mekki.

In addition to the council proper, the Executive Committee laid on the most extensive celebration of Nuba culture since the SPLA began organising in the Mountains. Dozens of groups came from every one of the seven counties to put on a show of a size unparalleled since Commander Kuwa began sponsoring a revival of Nuba cultures. The self-confident expression of Nuba culture is an integral part of the agenda of liberation.

There was wrestling, stick fighting, stilt-walking, singing, dancing and an extraordinarily wide range of music played on a variety of old and new instruments. After the festival, dancing continued into the small hours (with ordinary women and girls showing no hesitation in inviting Commander Yousif Kuwa to dance, and the commander showing no hesitation in accepting.) One delegate from Heiban said it was the first time he had been able to see the dances of the western jebels.

How Democratic is the Council?

The question of the independence of the Advisory Council from the SPLA and Commander Kuwa was raised at its first meeting in 1992 by Commander Telefon Kuku, who criticised Kuwa for speaking out in the debate on whether to continue the war. Kuwa explained, Telefon said I should not have spoken; people were afraid of me. I said to him, "My friend, in a democratic parliament everyone is free to voice their opinions." And I told him, "Whether I am democratic or not, I am more democratic than you." He used to beat soldiers for beating him at cards. I have never beaten an officer or a soldier."

The climate at the Advisory Council reflected the generally good relations between civilians and soldiers in the mountains today. Although civilian delegates were not as vocal as military delegates, a number felt confident enough to criticise the behaviour of the SPLA in some parts of the Nuba Mountains. Complaints ranged from unequal distribution of relief supplies to the excessive dowry of five cows paid by Alternate Commander Mohamed Juma. (Despite Juma's high rank, three cows were confiscated by the council as soon as the complaint was voiced and returned to their original owner.) Commander Kuwa accepted the criticisms but said, "There are individual criticisms. It is important not to draw general conclusions. Officers must treat civilians correctly, but each man must stand up for his own rights and call a spade a spade. Justice begins at home."

Governor Yousif Kuwa is a commanding figure, a confident, charismatic man who enjoys great popularity with ordinary people. The Advisory Council was his creation. He commands the men who carry the guns. Yet it was not Kuwa but Musa Abdel Bagi Fadel, a medical assistant, who called the shots as Chairman of the Advisory Council. Abdel Bagi did not hesitate to call the Governor to order when he saw fit. Towards the end of the assembly, for example, Kuwa took the microphone to suggest that delegates vote on a national tree for the Nuba. Abdel Bagi requested that he return to his seat because the issue of a national tree was not on the council's agenda and could be discussed at another time. "Our parliament is based on democracy," he explained later. "I am chairman of the Advisory Council. Yousif Kuwa is an ordinary member and should not force his ideas on other people. The question of the tree could be discussed in another place."

Abdel Bagi's authority was boosted by Kuwa's deference-a deference rate in any armed leader and especially in an SPLA commander.

George Boutros, a human rights monitor, remarked: "People are not afraid to speak. In 1992, really there were mistakes in the SPLA and people did not feel so free. But since we made our civilian organisation, everybody understands each other. Everything now is OK." Father Renato Kizito said:

At times it may appear like a bit of a show. But I think and hope I do not exaggerate to say that here the SPLA is really the expression of the people. Most of the people that I know that are in the SPLA are villagers who took up arms to defend their own family, to defend their own village. So they are concerned about the people. They know that without the support of the people they would be wiped away in no time. At the beginning it was maybe slightly different, from what I've heard from the people. Or very different at the very beginning, when in some villages the SPLA was seen as an occupation army like the government army. But now the situation has drastically changed for the better.

The Meeting Opens

In typical Nuba fashion, the Advisory Council opened with readings from the Koran and the Bible by the most senior Moslem cleric in the Mountains, Imam Adam Tutu Atrun, and a representative of the New Sudan Council of Churches, Father Butros Sanaba. There followed a minute's silence for the victims of the war. Then the Secretary of the Advisory Council, Bilel Abdel Rahman, urged delegates to "speak freely, with open hearts and minds".

The days of the debate that followed lacked the focal point of many previous Advisory Councils, for example the vote on whether to continue the war in 1992, the establishment of a Religious Tolerance Conference in 1994. The second half was dominated by the presence, and the lengthy and sometimes repetitive speeches, of the

Nuba visitors from abroad. Discussion was rather shallow, with little debate. A failing many delegates acknowledged and attributed to the problems of education in the Mountains. Hamad Brema, medical assistant, said:

> Democracy needs educated people who know their rights and the importance of voting. This is not a genuine democracy because people are lacking in education and the majority do not know what a genuine democracy is. The great task on the shoulders of the government is education. The little people feel free to speak, but often don't have anything to say because of the lack of education.

> Not just lack of education; also lack of information. Because the isolation of the mountain, and the difficulty of disseminating information in the region which does not have even a radio station, the Advisory Council serves as an information office at least as much as a decision-making body. Governor Kuwa, for example, used the Council to brief delegates on the latest in the talks between the Sudan Government and the SPLA. His reading of the opposition National Democratic Alliance "Asmara Declaration" held delegates spellbound.

The will behind the Council was remarkable. The benches were full well in advance of the beginning of every session and there was no coming and going at all. There is no doubt that this was a major event for the participants, and a morale-booster.

The council is a rare opportunity to bring Nuba together from all over the mountains. Much of the work went on in evening meetings on the sidelines of the Council, in which the Governor and administrators talked with leaders of the seven counties about developments and problems in their areas. In this way, the Council served to inform the leadership about local developments, as much as it served to inform the delegates about wider events.

Evaluating the SPLM

The first agenda item was the evaluation of the SPLM administration and political experience in the Nuba Mountains. This was discussed on the first day. Relief was the main topic of interest and many delegates were critical of the relief programme run by NRRDO. The first speaker, Abu Zeid Jos, of Delami County, accused the SPLA/M of "cheating the people". He said relief was not reaching the needy. The arrival of planes carrying aid was a big success for the armed struggle but the aid was not being distributed properly. Hammad Dar Juad, of Dilling County, agreed. He said there might be greater fairness, and improved morale in the ranks of the SPLA, if soldiers had uniforms and shoes. Simon Noah, human rights monitor, urged fair distribution of relief regardless of personal and tribal interests. He cautioned against reliance on relief. Elias Abdel Rahim, of Lagawa County, said cooperation between civilians and soldiers was good. But he said officials were making decisions that could not be implemented. Hammad Brema warned that a lack of accountability threatened corruption. He said it was up to the Advisory Council to establish accountability since the Council had established the NRRDO.

In response Yousif Kuwa said there was not enough relief to go all round. He ordered the SPLA/M to "treat the people properly" and warned that "tribal" habits would sow the seeds of disunity.

There were also comments on to SPLM administration in general. El Amin Dafaala urged mutual respect between the SPLA and the people. The army was fighting for people and should not mistreat them. Being a soldier was not an end in itself; it was a means to an end: winning back lost rights. Mariam Yohanna-the most vocal of the women delegates-criticised the Advisory Council for failing to implement its recommendations. She cited decisions about the care of widows, orphans and the disabled. "Be serious!" she said.

Musa Abdel Bagi responded that most decisions were implemented. Those that were not, were not because of the security situation. Governor Kuwa gave a historical resume, concluding, "We have taken up arms because of a political decision" to redress the injustice of Khartoum's development policies. He said that the civil administration was in its infancy and would become more efficient. "We still need experience. But let us all believe in democracy. Then we will succeed."

Future Directions

The second agenda item was the strategic future policy of the SPLM and the ways of confronting Sudan Government's policies. In this discussion, SPLA members made most of the interventions. The dominant themes were distrust of the NDA (National Democratic Alliance) and support for re-activation of Komolo (Youth) a clandestine political movement founded in the late 1970s by a group of Nuba from Khartoum University including Yousif Kuwa to represent the Nuba, in preference to the approach of the older generation of Nuba politicians.

There seem to be two main reasons for the new interest in the Komolo. First, both the government and opposition were talking of a referendum on the future shape of Sudan, in which, according to the SPLA, the Nuba will have the chance to vote for self-determination alongside Southern Sudanese. Second, the disintegration of the Sudan National Party (the principal civilian Nuba Party) and the death of its chairman Hassan el Mahi had left a political vacuum for the Nuba who were not in the SPLM-administered areas. Distrust of the NDA was founded in the experience of the "democratic" government of 1986-9, dominated by the main parties now in the NDA, which was a time of serious abuses against the Nuba.

The revitalisation of Komolo is potentially a very important step for the Nuba. However, in general there was little genuine debate about the options for the Nuba in the future, but instead a reiteration of long-held fears of marginalisation and repression.

There was also a discussion and a vote on the conditions under which an Operation Lifeline Sudan assessment team could be received in the mountains. There was a unanimous vote that it had to be headed by someone from the southern sector, departing from Lokichokkio in Kenya and not Khartoum, and could not include any Sudanese member.

Policies Adopted

The third agenda item concerned the recommendations of the Executive Committee, which had been drawn up in advance of the Council. These were approved in their entirety.

In the sphere of politics, the chief recommendation was to encourage the re-establishment of the Komolo organisation. Only one concrete recommendation was made by the Council, namely that training centres be established. Other recommendations included creating political commissars to educate the military and encouraging Nuba abroad and in garrison towns to join the movement.

In the social sphere, there was a vigorous debate on the question of bridewealth. The Executive Committee recommended increasing the maximum dowry value of cows from 6000 to 15000 Sudanese pounds, and of goats from 500 to 3000. A range of different proposals were put forward from abolition of bridewealth (from a female delegate) to removing the regulation of bridewealth altogether. However the initial proposal was adopted in the end.

Other recommendations included training women in handicrafts and housekeeping, and establishing an institute to further these skills, and educating people about the role of women in society and women's rights.

The Council also discussed the issue of divorce for women whose husbands were off fighting in the South. The Council agreed it was difficult to sanction divorce in these cases because the husbands were in a mission and were unable to speak for themselves. There was a suggestion that "temporary marriages" should be possible. It was agreed that the matter should be referred to the judicial seminar, to be convened in December.

Concerning administration, the first proposal was to encourage civilians not to neglect their own work in order to serve the military. Soldiers must cultivate their own plots and not rely on food from civilians. An earlier decision to establish cooperative farms in each village to support communal efforts was repeated.

Debate focussed on a proposal to divide one of the seven counties into two separate counties, but the Council voted against, on the ground that the division would necessarily be along tribal lines and this would increase the possibility of tribal conflict.

On economic issues, the Council voted to build up grain reserves against the threat of famine. There was also a discussion on the opening of markets to Arabs. The issue was referred to the Council's economic sub-committee, which would recommend to the Executive Committee (1) the safest place for a market with Arabs, (2) the funding of the wholesale purchases at a safe place outside the mountains and (3) details of a trade agreement exchanging crops for other commodities.

There was some discussion on health and the Committee's proposals were adopted, namely to institute home visits by health workers to advise on first aid and basic hygiene, and to warn against the dangers of HIV/AIDS.

Concerning education, there was a debate on the languages to be used. The demands of communication made it important to use Arabic, but the delegates were also determined to keep alive the many traditional Nuba languages. It was decided to teach local languages in schools but keep the medium of instruction as Arabic. However the history of the Nuba should be re-written, from a Nuba perspective, and taught in schools.

Concerning the judiciary, the maximum levels of fines that could be imposed by the courts were increased.

The Nuba from abroad

For the Nuba in the Mountains, a major highlight of the Council was the presence of Nuba from abroad, especially Suleiman Musa Rahhal of Nuba Mountains Solidarity Abroad. The three foreign delegates-Suleiman Rahhal, Suleiman Bakheit and Nur Tawir Kafi-all spoke at length about the situation of the Nuba outside and the political position of the Nuba vis-à-vis the NDA. "There is a political vacuum for the Nuba," said Suleiman Rahhal.

While these speeches imparted nothing new to the foreign attendees, they were a strong symbolic gesture to the Nuba inside, cut off for so long. Musa Abdel Bagi said: "It is very important that people see people coming from outside, we are really cut off. We need the solidarity of others who will convey our message to the Nuba outside and to the international community." Hammad Brema added:

"The Advisory Council was important because for the first time delegates came from abroad. All this time we have been engaged in the struggle, concerned that we are not representing the majority of the Nuba people. We ask ourselves: Are we really doing what the Nuba want? We have that fear. The answer we got from them is that the majority abroad supports us."

Yousif Kuwa's Speech

The sixth agenda item was the concluding speech by Governor Yousif Kuwa. He stressed the importance of the delegates from abroad, and went on to a historical resume: "History teaches us that Sudan is an Arab country and slaves traders of

Zubeir Pasha are "heroes." As a result the Nuba lost their confidence and fell into two groups: house boys and field workers. "The house boys ate the food of their masters, grew fat and despised the others."

On the current political situation, Yousif Kuwa stressed the weight of the Nuba in the SPLA. He read the Asmara declaration and stressed that it gave the Nuba and Southern Blue Nile the chance of a referendum to choose whether to join the South or follow a different path. He said that the Sudan Government was militarily weak, relying on conscripting students to fight the war.

Yousif Kuwa touched on the fact that the Nuba war is becoming a war of Nuba against Nuba, with the Sudan Government putting Nuba troops in the front line.

The majority of the soldiers in the garrisons are Nuba. We must formulate policies to counter this. Since colonisation the government has depended on the Nuba. Now we are fighting for ourselves. We must talk to them (the garrison Nuba), convince them. The government is telling them: You won't be able to dance in the Nuba Mountains. Our civil administration must get the truth to the garrisons. We must tell them: here you can cultivate and dance freely. So at the very least they do not attack us and steal our cows.

The acting chairman then called for debate on the Governor's speech, but this was pre-empted by Nur Tawir Kafi who took the floor to explain her position at length. This used up the time allocated for discussion, leaving only enough time for Yousif Kuwa to thank delegates and tell them: "If things go according to plan, the next meeting will be in Kadugli. Tell the people and prepare yourselves for Kadugli!"

After the meeting ended, Governor Kuwa commented: "All I can hope for is that my general principles filter down to the people. I feel I am not a commander. I do not feel I am a leader. I only feel I am a teacher whose objective is to tell the people what is right and how to get their rights."

Follow-Up

After the Council ended, the secretary, Bilal Abdel Rahman, hand-copied the final resolutions, which covered several pages, 55 times for distribution across the mountains. At some of the earlier Council meetings no paper was available-such was the scarcity of basic items due to the government blockade-and the resolutions could not be recorded in writing.

Much of the work of detailing and implementing the resolutions fell to the subcommittees of the Executive Committee, especially the economic and the judicial subcommittees. The work of these committees will be an important test of the effectiveness of the civil administration and the democratic accountability of the Advisory Council system.

12

Unity in Diversity: Is it Possible in Sudan?

Ahmed Ibrahim Diraige

Sudan is the largest country in Africa and Middle East. It is the ninth largest country in the world and from North to South extends from latitude 22N to 4N. It has a diversity of climates. As you go from north to South you move from desert environment through semi-desert, savannah to sub-tropical and tropical climate. This kind of environment has created a diverse pattern of economic and social life.

The population of Sudan is made up of over 500 tribes divided into two distinct ethnicity-Arab and non-Arab. From the religious point of view there are Moslems, Christians and those who follow native religions. The country was originally made up of ancient indigenous and tribal homelands which have subsequently been brought together by various colonial forces into the present Sudanese State.

Thus we can see that Sudan is a country of several diversities, ethnic, religious, cultural and regional. During colonial rule, peace and stability were maintained throughout Sudan.

But these ethnic and regional diversities began to emerge again after independence in 1956, resulting in a civil war in the South and dissatisfaction in the peripheries of the North. The war in the South has continued intermittently up to this day, while the regional discontent in the North has developed into armed resistance against the state.

These facts have led many people to ask the question: is unity in the

Sudan possible given such diversity?

In my view, unity is not only possible but is imperative. Even before colonial times, the various indigenous kingdoms and tribal homelands were associated with each other in different ways. The colonial period brought these regions together under one administration and subsequent governments cemented the loose relations that previously existed among the component parts of Sudan.

The economic and political conditions of the world today favour a bigger association of nations rather than the disintegration of the component parts of a living state. Therefore the possibility of the Sudan remaining as one country in spite of the present problems is possible.

What is needed to maintain this unity is a clear understanding that Sudan is a country of diverse religious, cultural, ethnic and regional people, and that these diversities should be mutually respected by all the Sudanese groups.

What happened after independence is that those who inherited political power from the colonial forces refused to recognise and respect the diversity of the Sudan. Instead they only recognised the Arab and Moslem culture and refused to recognise the non-Moslem and non-Arab cultures. They also refused to accept a decentralised system of government, which would have been better placed to accommodate the regional diversity of the country.

Today we are on the verge of making a constitution for the Sudan after the fall of the present government. If we can incorporate what has been accepted by all the Sudanese opposition forces in 1995 during the Asmara Conference as parameters for the New Sudanese constitution, peace will prevail and the unity of Sudan will be achieved inclusive of all its diversity.

13

What Peace for the Nuba?

Suleiman Musa Rahhal

The war in Sudan has been going on for seventeen years. For all its victims, it has been a brutal and miserable experience. But among all the suffering people of Sudan, the Nuba stand out as a people who have been on the frontline for fifteen years, exposed to the atrocities of the Sudan government forces and the deprivations of famine without any respite. The Nuba also stand out as a people who have been ignored by the international community. Their basic needs unmet and their cries for help unheard.

Recently, there have been important peace initiatives in Sudan. During 1999, the IGAD countries and their western donors reinvigorated the IGAD forum with the intent of finding peace in Southern Sudan. This is a forum in which the SPLM meets the Sudan Government. Simultaneously, the Libyan and Egyptian governments launched their own initiative for peace, supported by most of the northern political parties. Where, ask the Nuba people, do we stand in these crucial initiatives?

There is a long and sorry history of the Nuba voice being excluded from national and international initiatives to achieve peace in Sudan. No Nuba representatives were able to attend the meeting of Atlanta, Georgia, on 8 January 1992. Neither were any present for the Nairobi Declaration (religion and state) of 17 April 1993, the Washington Declaration of October 1993, the IGAD Peace Talks of 1994, the Cairo Agreement of June 1994, the Chukudum Agreement of December 1994, and the Barcelona Conference of October 1995. The Nuba were not represented at any of these conferences; in a bitter recollection of their past exclusion.

The Nuba voice in the Asmara Declaration of June 1995 was confined to the small delegation of the Sudan National Party—which only represents one part of the Nuba constituency. However Commander Yousif Kuwa was a member of the SPLM delegations to the Abuja talks in 1993 and the IGAD meetings of August 1998 and July 1999. But the Abuja meeting agreed only on self-determination for Southern Sudan, while the entire IGAD process is mainly focused on the South, with the Nuba and Southern Blue Nile as a footnote.

The IGAD Declaration of Principles (DOP) was adopted in 1994 as the basis for talks between the government and SPLA. Two months later, these six points were whittled down to two main points—a secular, democratic, united Sudan and, failing that, a referendum for the people of the South on the basis of self-determination. Initially, these two points were rejected outright by the government spokesman Ghazi Salah el-Din Attabani, who said both main points were unacceptable to Khartoum. The regime would not compromise either on its Islamic agenda or its refusal of self-determination for the South. This position was not negotiable. However, in 1997 the government returned to the negotiating table, accepting the DOP. The SPLM accepted to resume the negotiations on this basis. But the status of the Nuba and Southern Blue Nile still remained unclear. According to the Asmara Declaration and the IGAD DOP—both of which the SPLM has signed—the Nuba have no right to self-determination. But according to the proposal for a confederal system with a northern entity and a southern entity, tabled by the SPLM to IGAD in October 1997, the Nuba and Southern Blue Nile fall within an enlarged Southern Sudan. Under this proposal, the Nuba would only have the right of self-determination as part of a "greater" Southern Sudan, not in their own right.

The position of the government and the northern parties in the NDA is essentially the same. They have only reluctantly recognised the right of Southern Sudan for self-determination, and have completely stalled on the issue of the Nuba. In the December 1994 Chukudum Agreement, the Umma Party, recognised the right of the South for self-determination, but denied the Nuba that self-same right (Clause 4.2):

The Umma Party rejects the mention and inclusion of the Nuba Mountains, the Abyei Region and the Ingessena Hills in the self-determination clause because it does not recognise the right to self-determination for any group outside the Southern Sudan.

In a succession of agreements and declarations of principle, the Nuba people have been denied the right of self-determination. The Nuba would like to ask why they have been denied this basic right while it has been granted to the people of the South? What about the rights of the other marginalised people in Northern Sudan?

The question of self-determination is central to Nuba aspirations. It is important to understand the meaning of the word "self-determination" before discussing what it means to the Nuba. D. B. Levin in 1962 defined self-determination as "the rights of people of a nation to freely, without outside pressure, determine their state affiliation, including the rights to form an independent state and also to determine the forms their internal political, economic, social and cultural life, which is guaranteed by international organisations and bodies."

But self-determination, widely used today by many Sudanese politicians, has more than one interpretation. To some it means recognition of a basic individual right while to others it means "self-rule or government". To some Southerners as well as to some Northerners, it means the opt-out of the South with a new capital in Juba.

We can easily predict some aspects of the social and cultural life of a Southern state. There will be no Sharia, for example. But self-determination also means the right of a people to establish their own political system from top to bottom. This cannot happen overnight; it needs far more than a referendum.

In fact, the true meaning of self-determination is found when the people themselves take control of political decisions. If Sudan is to be truly democratic, the opposition forces must first have internal democracy. A good model for this is in the SPLA-held areas of the Nuba Mountains, which boasts the only democratically elected assembly anywhere in Sudan. If there is to be self-determination, it must arise from a process that enables people to acquire political education and experience so they can freely exercise their basic democratic rights. Only in the Nuba Mountains can people debate these matters freely and openly.

We cannot pre-judge the outcome. We all have our personal views. Some of us prefer unity. Some would like confederation with Darfur, and some want an independent state. The important thing is not the outcome; it is the process. It must be democratic and participatory. In the Nuba context, self-determination means first and foremost the right to be able to sit together and freely discuss all options, to know that whatever we decide, our democratic wishes will be respected.

The "Call of the Nation" signed by Sadiq el Mahdi and President Bashir in Djibouti in November 1999 is a step backwards for the Nuba. The "declaration of principles" is silent on religion and the state, clearly leaving the door open for an Islamic constitution. From the Nuba point of view, the main virtue of the agreement is its clarity: it specifically denies self-determination for the Nuba and Ingessena, instead offering them administrative autonomy within a united Sudan.

Any international mediator or facilitator in the Sudanese peace process has duties and responsibilities towards the Nuba. It should include the Nuba on its agenda for future discussion. Nuba representatives should attend all future negotiations. Failing to put the Nuba on the peace agenda will condemn the Nuba and their culture to a silent death. It will also imperil any peace agreement.

Despite the odds against them, the Nuba are resilient and determined to fight to the end. There will be no peace in Southern Kordofan until justice is done. Nuba land must be returned to its rightful owners and the Nuba's right to self-determination must be recognised. There is hope of peaceful co-existence between Nuba and Baggara, for the Baggara realise that they have been used by the regime in Khartoum. Peace agreements have recently been made between the Hawazma and the Nuba and between the Nuba and Rawouga Arab tribe. These agreements are perceived as threats by the government and Arab traders have become targets for armed forces who prevent them from entering SPLA-controlled areas of the Nuba Mountains.

Any peace agreement must also address the problems of marginalised people who live in Khartoum and the other cities of the North. Nuba, Southerners and people of Darfur are routinely discriminated against, given only dirty jobs refused by Arabs and paid pittances. This has caused considerable discomfort to many educated Nuba and has been additional motivation for the Nuba to join the SPLA's war of liberation.

The Nuba are not silent on these issues. One of the important lessons that the Nuba have learned from their long and bitter struggle is that they can rely only on themselves. As Yagoub Osman Kaloka of the Tira people has put it:

The Tira have learned enough from this war. They have come through the serious hunger and suffering of 1990-92, they have become well built-up. They can resist. They know how to defend their culture.[1]

This is true for peace as much as for war. Nuba leaders have therefore been at work, canvassing the opinions of the Nuba inside Sudan-both in the government-controlled and SPLM-administered areas-and in the diaspora, holding many meetings, and developing their proposals.

In December, 1998 Commander Yousif Kuwa Mekki, the Nuba leader and the Governor of South Kordofan met British Government Officials at the Foreign Office and Department of International Development. He clarified and articulated the Nuba position and the terms upon which Nuba would be prepared to lay down the arms for a comprehensive peace settlement. The full text is in Appendix 1. In outline, Commander Kuwa demanded that the Nuba people be awarded the right of self-determination in their own right. The Nuba should be given a separate but parallel deal to that offered for Southern Sudan. All the provisions for interim administration, human rights and democracy, and self-determination that are awarded to Southern Sudan should also be awarded, separately and in parallel, to the Nuba. This position was widely supported by Nuba of all shades of political opinion. It represents the only truly fair and democratic means whereby the Nuba can determine their own destiny.

The second part of Commander Kuwa's position called for the Nuba Mountains to be provided with humanitarian aid from the international community, again on the same terms as it is provided to Southern Sudan. Since this call was made, there has been some progress. The UN finally sent an assessment mission to the Nuba Mountains in mid-1999. A second mission then travelled to look at how an assistance programme could be implemented. But, months later, no aid had been delivered, and in the 2000 dry season offensive, the Sudan Government made a concerted attempt to close the airstrips and cut off all aid access: the humanitarian situation still hangs in the balance.

Conclusion

It would be a fatal mistake for anyone to believe that peace in Sudan can be reached at the expense of the Nuba and other marginalised peoples in the North. As one of the speakers said at the Nuba International Conference in London on 20 April 1996:

It is the Nuba, two million African people in the heart of the country, who carry the flame for a brighter Sudan. If that flame is extinguished, we shall all pay the price.

There can be no peace without justice. If the political leaders of Sudan, the African and Arab countries and the international community as a whole believe that they can make peace in Sudan at the expense of the Nuba, they are mistaken. The Nuba will not settle for an agreement that does not guarantee their rights in full. It is not only a question of justice; it is a question of redistributing power. The Nuba have resisted the most ferocious onslaught of the Sudanese army and can do so again. But if we, the Nuba, are granted our rights, we will do our part to ensure that our region, Sudan and the whole of Africa is free, peaceful and democratic.

---

1 "Facing Genocide: The Nuba of Sudan". African Rights, 1995: Interview in Tira Limon, 23 May 1995.

Appendix 1

Clarifications on the SPLM Peace Position with Regard to the Nuba Mountains

Presented by Commander Yousif Kuwa Mekki
London, December 1998

The Political Position

1. The Nuba are part and parcel of the SPLA/M and are committed to the SPLA/M position on peace in Sudan presented to various IGAD meetings.

2. The Nuba strongly support the IGAD Declaration of Principles and the maturing IGAD peace process.

3. The Nuba are central to the Sudanese conflict and hold the key to vital questions of ethnic rights and religious tolerance.

4. The Nuba people demand the right of self-determination. The Nuba people are entitled to this international human right for the following reasons:

   4.1 Because of their long history of being treated as second-class citizens in Sudan.
   4.2 Because of the threat of genocide that hangs over them.
   4.3 Because of their long and bitter struggle for their right of justice and equality.

4.4 Because the right of self-determination has been recognised for Southern Sudan.

4.5 Because they were administered as a "closed district" along with Southern Sudan (and also Southern Blue Nile) from 1922 onwards.

5. The Nuba right to self-determination must be recognised to achieve a genuine and comprehensive settlement to the long-running conflict in Sudan.

6. The Nuba are not demanding secession. The Nuba demand the right to choose in their own right.

7. The Nuba's preferred option is the unity of the Sudan, with the Nuba enjoying full self-government within a decentralised system.

8. During the interim period between the signing of a Peace Agreement and the final exercise of self-determination, the Nuba demand the following:

8.1 To be treated equally with south Sudan and in parallel in any peace deal.
8.2 Interim self-administration of the Nuba Mountains under the SPLA/M on the same terms as South Sudan.
8.3 A secular, pluralist and democratic regional administration.
8.4 International guarantees for the future of the Nuba as an integral part of any peace deal from the outset.
8.5 The presence to ensure respect of human rights and the free and fair conduct of the exercise of the right of self-determination.
8.6 The Nuba people will exercise their international monitors to right of self-determination separately after the people of Southern Sudan have made their decision in an internationally-monitored referendum.

9. The Nuba respect the inalienable right of the people of Southern Sudan to self-determination. The future of Southern Sudan is a matter for Southern Sudanese.

9.1 The Nuba would prefer for the South to remain in a united Sudan. But in the case of the people of Southern Sudan opting through a democratic process to secede from Sudan, the Nuba will respect that choice.

9.2 In the case of the people of Southern Sudan opting for separation in the exercise of their right to self-determination, the Nuba will have the following options:
   (i). To choose to be part of Southern Sudan state, or
   (ii). To choose to be part of the Northern Sudan state, or
   (iii). To choose to have an independent statehood.

10. The Nuba call for the implementation of impartial relief and development programmes during the interim period.

11. Both the humanitarian and political positions narrated in this Clarification apply to the people of Southern Blue Nile. Southern Blue Nile is therefore entitled to a deal on the same terms as the Nuba.

The Humanitarian Position

1. The Nuba people are in a critical humanitarian situation. Our people are still dying of hunger and disease, as well as from government attacks, landmines and aerial bombardment including cluster bombs.

2. The Sudanese government continues to deny access to UN humanitarian relief agencies despite a promise to UN Secretary General Kofi Annan in May 1998 to allow Operation Lifeline Sudan (OLS) to go to the Nuba Mountains.

APPENDIX 2

Resolutions of the Conference What Peace for the Nuba?

London 1996

The International Nuba conference, "What Peace for the Nuba?" issued the following call to the international community and the people of Sudan:

The plight of the Nuba illustrates many dimensions of the conflict in Sudan, and if we are seeking a long-lasting solution to the problems of the country as a whole, we cannot afford to ignore the Nuba.

The opposition groups such as the NDA and SPLA must recognise that they cannot take Nuba support for granted in their struggle against the destructive totalitarianism of the National Islamic Front regime. They cannot regard the Nuba as mere pawns in the civil war.

Instead, they must recognise that the questions raised by the treatment of the Nuba in the past must now be addressed, for the sake of the entire country. Other "marginalised" peoples in Sudan face the same fate.

The principal issues are:

1) Self-determination:

The need for genuinely democratic political representation for all communities, and an end to the centralised and exploitative methods of governments, past and present, in Sudan. The seeds of this democracy are already evident in the Nuba areas under the control of local people in SPLA- held territory.

The Nuba as well as other non-Arab peoples of Northern Sudan such as the Beja and the people of Darfur must be fully involved in the political process as equals. This is the true meaning of self-determination.

2) Land rights:

It is clear that the best custodians of the land are the indigenous people themselves, and not the elite groups who have gained control of the large areas of land through political favouritism. The Nuba farmers are forced to become dispossessed labourers on massive mechanised agricultural schemes, which is an abuse not only of human and economic rights, but also of the fertile land on which the country depends.

The abuse of mechanised agriculture has only brought destruction to the fragile soils of South Kordofan. This has gone on too long, with international bodies working as accomplices with absentee landlords to the maximise profits while accelerating ecological devastation. The process is only adding fuel to the conflict, and must be halted. Instead, there must be respect for the knowledge of local farmers, whose techniques are most likely to maintain sustainable agricultural development.

This is absolutely crucial element which the government and opposition have shown no sign of understanding.

3) Religion:

In a society as diverse and complex as Sudan, state and religion must be separated to avoid discrimination and corruption. The Nuba have been victimised regardless of their religious adherence, and have discovered at painful cost, that conversion to Islam has not protected them from racial discrimination, gross human exploitation, and from being robbed of their land.

On the contrary, because the Nuba community has shown that Muslims, Christians and followers of traditional religion can co-exist peacefully, they have aroused the anger of those who practice division and intolerance in the name of Islam.

Since the majority of Sudanese, from North and South, do not accept the

National Islamic Front's claims to represent Islam, they instead look to the Nuba for an example of more positive, compassionate approach to religious belief and its role in society.

It is the Nuba, two million African people in the heart of the country, who carry the flame for a brighter future in Sudan. If that flame is extinguished, we all pay the price.

Appendix 3

A list of Nuba citizens arrested and extra judicially executed by the Military Intelligence Service of the Sudan government

Name	Occupation	Tribe	Age	Arrest/Execution
1. Ramadan Agabana	DPW[1]	Miri	38	Oct/1988
2. Mohammed Ali Musa	Clerk	Temein	35	Aug/1990
3. El-Haj A/Aziz Tiya	UWA[2]	Damik	35	Aug/1990
4. Abdalla Omda	Vet. Nurse	Korongo	30	Aug/1990
5. Ibrahim Marmatoon	CEC[3]	Kadugli	24	Aug/1990
6. Mohammed Nafa'	driver	Abuhasheem	25	Aug/1990
7. Musa Kibbi	med.worker	Abuhasheem	30	Aug/1990
8. Abdalla Kafi	med.worker	Kadugli	51	Aug/1990
9. Musa Ismail A/Gadir	med.officer	Kadugli	47	Aug/1990
10 Sabir Abrian	farmer	Moro	46	Aug/1990
11 Ali Tona Tiya	farmer	Moro	35	Aug/1990
12 Kamal Kano Kafi	radio tech.	Kaduli	25	Aug/1990
13 Al-Tagani M.Shukrala	ass.dentist	Kagugli	27	Aug/1990
14 Ibrahim Gadraibak	nurse	Kadugli	31	Aug/1990
15 Osman Dawood	farmer	Kawalib	32	03/08/90
16 Omer Ahmed A/Fatah	worker	Kawalib	37	08.09.90
17 Fadelel-Mula Haroun	worker	Kawalib	35	08.09.90
18 Saad Ali Idris	worker	Kawalib	36	08.09.90
19 Ibrahim Komi	farmer	Kawalib	40	08.09.90
20 Ibrahim Noli	farmer	Kawalib	35	08.09.90
21 Mohamed Ali A/Alla	farmer	Kawalib	38	08.09.90
22 Hussein Abdalla	farmer	Kawalib	35	08.09.90
23 Saeed Koko	farmer	Kawalib	31	08.09.90
24 Idris Koko	farmer	Kawalib	26	08.09.90
25 Khalifa Koko	farmer	Kawalib	30	08.09.90
26 Ahamed Sanddog	farmer	Kawalib	32	08.09.90
27 Al-Fiel Konda	farmer	Kawalib	37	08.09.90
28 Ayoub Mahjoub	farmer	Kawalib	36	08.09.90
29 Osman Abdel-Gadir	farmer	Kawalib	35	08.09.90
30 Hassan Diggais Mursal	farmer	Miri	45	08.09.90
31 Ali Kowa	farmer	Miri	43	08.09.90
32 Hassan Mohamed Kakki	farmer	Miri	65	08.09.90
33 Hassan Bakheit Kakki	farmer	Miri	45	08.09.90

34	Salih Ali Abrahim	farmer	Miri	28	08.09.90
35	Ja'afar Abdalla	farmer	Miri	21	08.09.90
36	Sabit Mansour	farmer	Miri	35	08.09.90
37	Mikaeil Hassab Idris	farmer	Miri	32	08.09.90
38	Ibrahim Abusadur	farmer	Kawalib	50	08.09.90
39	Daffa'alla Nima	farmer	Kawalib	40	08.09.90
40	Hussein Kacho	shepherd	Kawalib	35	08.09.90
41	Ahmed Nawai	farmer	Kadro	48	Aug/1990
42	Birair Khalifa Bakheit	teacher	Jaroro	29	14/10/90
43	Omer Ibrahim Kanno	analyst	Kamda	36	14/10/90
44	Hamdan Hassan Kouri	solicitor	Sabouri	27	14/10/90
45	Hassan Kouri Bakheit	prison officer	Sabouri	64	14/10/90
46	Mohamed Mekki Koko	engineer	Keiga	35	19/10/90
47	Eisa Kamdo	mechanic	Kadero	31	19/10/90
48	Sayid Hamid al-Daw	accountant	Taffarei	33	20/12/90
49	Nurel-Din Tia A/Gadir	driver	Murta	40	Oct/1990
50	Zakaria Hassan Musaa'd	merchant	Sabouri	40	14/10/90
51	Mozzamil Dabiyo Zayid	textile tech.	Kamda	28	14/10/90
52	Bilal Hamid Toto	teacher	Dalloka	35	14/10/90
53	Abuzaid Shalal Kowa	teacher	Murta	34	20/12/90
54	Ismat Hassan khirel-Seid	teacher	Kadugli	32	20/12/90
55	Yousif Saboun	teacher	Kadugli	35	14/10/90
56	Yousif Jaldakoun	teacher	Nyimang	34	14/10/90
57	Osman Adam Ali	agriculturist	Dilling	45	21/10/90
58	Sayid Ismail Kanno	teacher	Kadugli	36	21/10/90
59	Al-Nur Ismail Jarro	agr.researcher,	Lima	37	21/10/90
60	Al-Sir Abdel Nabi Malik	employer	Kadugli	29	21/10/90
61	Musa Ismail Rahhal	med.assistant	Kadugli	45	21/10/90
62	Ramadan Adam	med.commissioner,	Kadugli	31	14/10/90
63	A/Rahim Jadalla Kambal	field inspector,	Kadugli	40	14/10/90
64	Al-Zubair Dawood	gov.employee,	Kadugli	32	14/10/90
65	Ismail Hassan A/Razig	soldier	Kadugli	25	14/10/90
66	Ahmed Suleiman Ajib	NMAC[4]	Dilling	35	14/10/90
67	Dawood Al-Sakin	radio technician,	Moro	28	14/10/90
68	Ali Osman	construction dept,	Lagori	33	14/10/90
69	Ali Bashir	construction corp,	Lagawa	34	14/10/90
70	Ismail Adam	nurse	Korongo	31	14/10/90
71	Ali Anglo	agr.reseach corp,	Miri	34	14/10/90
72	Ali Osman	nurse	Moro	25	14/10/90
73	Hassan Abdalla Idris	nurse	Moro	38	14/10/90
74	Osman Tiya	construction corp,	Kadugli	40	14/10/90
75	Abu-Ras Ibrahim	ex-trade unionist,	Kadero	48	Apr/90
76	Musa Kafi Toto	worker	Kadero	48	Apr/90
77	Abdalla Adam	merchant	Sabouri	45	Nov/90
78	Ahmed al-Badawi Yousif	construction corp,	Miri	35	Nov/90
79	Ahmed Omer Koko	postman	Saraf	32	Nov/90
80	Al-Nial Kazzama	travel agent	Moro	50	Nov/90
81	Alfaki Aburagala	nurse	Moro	37	Nov/90
82	Toto Armis	health officer	Katcha	34	Nov/90

#	Name	Occupation	Location	Age	Date
83	Sakken Tiya	educ. worker	Katcha	40	Nov/90
84	Mohammed A/Alla Garnas,	school super.	Kadugli	35	Nov/90
85	Rajab Adam	roneo tech.	Lima	38	20/10/90
86	Mohamed Eisa Ismail	sec., KTTU[5]	Kadugli	36	21/10/90
87	Abdalla Alla-Jabo	teacher	HagarAlmak	37	21/10/90
88	Kamal Nurel-Din Tiya	driver	Kadugli	38	14/10/90
89	Hamid Ghabbosh	driver	Kadugli	45	14/12/90
90	Mohamed Ali	clerk	Temin	40	
91	Mohamed Saboun	teacher	Kadugli	30	
92	Mohamed Nuwar Asso	dentist	Kadugli	45	
93	Mohamed Yahia	teacher	Tagali	28	
94	Abdulla Khalil	clerk	Miri	28	
95	Omer Ibrahim Kano	technician	Kadugli	29	
96	Suleiman Ismail	teacher	Muglad	32	
97	El-Ehaimir Kurtaila	merchant	Muglad	35	
98	Abushur Ali	farmer	Dilling	50	
99	Kurtobair Basha	Mek tribal chief,	Muglad	70	
100	Makina Khabar	farmer	Timatig	80	
101	Ebrahim Basha	retailer	Muglad	47	
102	Omer Laban	farmer	Shawayia	75	
103	Barashot Koko	farmer	Kuwalib	85	
104	Mohamed Hamad	farmer	El-Sawayia	24	
105	Mohamed Haroni	farmer	Kartago	21	
106	Ismail Sultan	farmer	Temin	32	
107	A/Rahim Shawayia	farmer	El-Shawayia	70	
108	Abdalla Hamad	sheikh	Tulishi	70	
109	Maki Tio	sheikh	Tulishi	65	
110	Bashir Kafi	sheikh	Tulishi	50	
111	Musa Kuwa	sheikh	Tulishi	56	
112	Koko Alyias	sheikh	Tulishi	44	
113	Mekki El-Mangoh	sheikh	Tulishi	60	
114	Abdel-Gadir Tia	sheikh	Tulishi	70	
115	Birisa Tia	sheikh	Tulishi	55	
116	Asta Ahmed	farmer	El-Khalgan	45	
117	Bashir Khalifa	farmer	El-Khalgan	33	
118	Esmail El-Daw	farmer	El-Khalgan	29	
119	Yousif Aboud	farmer	El-Khalgan	23	
120	Abdulla Aboud	farmer	El-Khalgan	25	
121	Eisa Ahmed	farmer	El-Khalgan	30	
122	Sultan Dahia Musa	sultan	Kamda	50	
123	Salih Ahmed A/Digin	omda	Kamda	47	
124	Adam Idris Adam	farmer	Kamda	40	
125	Shukr Alia Namla	farmer	Kamda	30	
126	Milim Hamad	policeman	Kamda	28	
127	Saboun Ahmed Saboun	retired soldier	Kamda	unknown	
128	Sayed Kabashi Kuwa	farmer	Kamda	30	
129	Abass Gangai Fadlalla	farmer	Kamda	45	
130	Adam Bakhiet	farmer	Kamda	50	
131	Omer El-Faki Ali	businessman	Kamda	45	

132 Ali Mohamed Faki Ali	businessman	Kamda	25
133 Mohamed Bakheit	businessman	Kamda	25
134 Eshak Mahil	businessman	Kamda	25
135 Abdulla Rajab Somi	nurse	Kamda	
136 Adam Ibrahim	farmer	Kaiga El-Kheil	25
137 Abu Rafas	farmer	Kaiga El-Kheil	23
138 Ahmed El-Nour Koko	teacher	Kandurma Teera,	24
139 Sherif	health worker	Abu Hashim	24
140 Mousa Tia	tailor	Abu Hashim	26
141 Khalifa Tia	sheikh	Shatt Faro	35
142 Hussein Tia	farmer	Shatt Faro	27
143 Othman Tia	farmer	Katcha	22
144 Toko Trfan	retailer	Shatt El-Damam	32
145 Harasa Mugood	farmer	Katcha	21
146 Suleiman Daldum	farmer	Daloka	45
147 Ali Thana	nurse	Blinga	33
148 Leti	farmer	El-Mogoro	27
149 Abred Ves	teacher	Shororo	33
150 Musa El-Zubeir	med. assistant	Kaiga Dameek,	23
151 Adam Ebrahim	agr. inspector Kaiga	Dameek,	29
152 El-Zubeir Dawood	water res.empl.	Lagori	27
153 Mohamed Abu Sitta	sheikh of Kalimo	Kadugli	60
154 Ibrahim Marmaton	admin worker	Kadugli	35
155 Jemi	agri. institute	Kadugli	26
156 Eisa Kajo	educ. dept	Heiban	30
157 Ahmed Yousif	public work	Kadugli	30
158 Ramadan Ajabna	const. worker	Miri	29
159 A/Al-Omda Sayed	vet.med.ass	Korongo	28
160 Kwal	retailer	Abyei	30
161 Koko Kani	worker	El-Buram	27
162 Suleiman Tot Kora	shepherd	El-Moro	35
163 Mohamed Silk	farmer	El-Moro	35
164 A/Rahman Habila	farmer	El-Moro	23
165 Hamdaig Shio	farmer	El-Khalgan	23
166 Ahmed El-Badawi	agri.inst. worker	Miri	29
167 Sikeen	school worker	Katcha	21
168 Mirghani Kafi	school worker	El-Kawalib	25
169 Batris Abdulla	farmer	El-Kawalib	23
170 Ahmed Suleiman	agri.inst. worker	Miri	29
171 El-Neil Karama	businessman	Moro el-Atmor	50
172 Ibrahim Abdel Gadir	hospital clerk	Kadugli	25
173 Mohammed Mekki Koko	worker	Lagori	23
174 Mohamed Suleiman	worker	Kamda	30
175 Muhi el-Dein Tia A/Qadir	driver	Kadugli/Murta	31
176 Muzamil Dyba El-Zein	factory worker	Kamda	28
177 Ramadan Adam Koko	hospital clerk	Kadugli	20
178 Osman Adam Ali	farmer	Kamda	22
179 Rajab Adam Mohamed	farmer	Kamda	25
180 Zakaria Hussein Kodi	teacher	Heiban	33

181 Geiberil Malakal	sheikh	Timen	43
182 El-Sheikh Shira	sheikh	Timen	35
183 Sabahi Malakal	farmer	Timen	42
184 Kold Famis	farmer	Timen	42
185 Koko Arbaa Hamir Mudari	farmer	Fama	34
186 Todwaa Koko	farmer	Fama	33
187 Kafi Fajita	farmer	Fama	29
188 Tia Jam	farmer	Fama	26
189 Kowa Kafi	sheikh of Fama	Fama	23
190 Driro Tia	farmer	Fama	39
191 Famaira Kano	farmer	Fama	21
192 Koko Jatrab	farmer	Fama	33
193 El-Tagadum Limr Ali	farmer	Fama	21
194 Tarbila Toto	farmer	Fama	26
195 Tshisha Koko	farmer	Fama	21
196 Kaka Toto	farmer	Fama	19
197 Hilina Kiki	housewife	Fama	17
198 Tojo Koko	housewife	Fama	21
199 Kaka Tiru	housewife	Fama	21
200 Kaki Yelow	housewife	Fama	23
200 Kaki Yelow	housewife	Fama	20
201 Koko Stri	farmer	Shatt el-Sifaya	25
202 Rahal Tims	farmer	Shatt el-Sifaya	27
203 Kafi Garboya	farmer	Shatt el-Sifaya	26
204 Kowa El-Eaisir	farmer	Shatt el-Sifaya	22
205 Toto Felaiga	farmer	Shatt el-Sifaya	25
206 El-Tanai Filaiga	farmer	Shatt El-Sifaya	25
207 Majo Kowi	farmer	Shatt El-Sifaya	25
208 Mrs Toto Boy	farmer	Shatt El-Sifaya	22
209 Ahemd Omewr Koko	post office	Kobs-Kadugli	29
210 Ahmed Shilin	tailor	Kadugli	33
211 Ezz El-Dein	teacher	Kawalib	25
212 Sheikh Hamdeen	Sheikh of Kiringa	Kutla	45
213 Fadl Tirkawi	farmer	El-Khalgan	37
214 Gibriel Mansha	farmer	El-Khalgan	55
215 Kurtaila Amon	farmer	El-Khalgan	65
216 Suleiman Bukhari	farmer	El-Bargo	37
217 Esmail Ergeen	farmer	El-Khalgan	20
218 Otman Joghan	farmer	El-Khalgan	unknown
219 Yousif Abdallah	Mosque admin	Kawalib	unknown
220 El Angowingasi	teacher	Kawalib	unknown
221 Musa Kuwa Kafi	teacher	Moro	unknown
222 Kano El-Laho	teacher	El-Buram	unknown
223 Shorain Baba	farmer	El-Khalfan	unknown
224 Ibrahim Daldoum	farmer	El-Khalfan	unknown
225 Hamad Abdulla	farmer/sheikh, retailer	Taymeen	unknown
226 El-Jaili Kaftira	farmer/sheikh, retailer	Kawalib	unknown
227 Ahmed Adllan Ibrahim	clerk	Nimang	unknown
228 El-Amin El-Raika Bangor	teacher	Kawalib	unknown
229 Hussien Ali Jaafar	Dilling Techn.Inst.	Kawalib	unknown

230 Abass Klaika	soldier	Kawalib	unknown
221 El-Amin El-Raika	teacher	Dilling	unknown
222 Awadalla Ismail	teacher	Dilling	unknown
223 Suleiman Abo El-Amin	Islamic mission	Dilling	unknown
224 El-Hamid El- Dou	driver	Dilling	unknown
225 Bixaima Mamour	tailor	Dilling	unknown
226 Jaafar Salfor	retailer	Dilling	unknown
227 Abass George	Sudan Airways	Dilling	unknown
228 Mahdi Rahal	accountant	Dilling	unknown
229 Hamad Gadal	administrator	Dilling	unknown
230 Etisam Butrus	clerk	Heiban	unknown
231 Rahila Kanda KoKo	headmistress	Heiban	unknown
232 Nada Yunis Sindali	student	Heiban	unknown
233 Awatif Atron	student	Dilling	unknown
234 Bahria Atron	student	Dilling	unknown
235 Aida Aboud	student	Dilling	unknown
236 Zeinab Nimir	student	Dilling	unknown
237 Gida Khasham	housewife	Kuwalib	unknown
238 Jumma Abdul Gadir	clerk	Dilling	unknown
239 Adula Hamid Slam Darfo	clerk	Dilling	unknown
240 Ahmed Nasir Basha	teacher	Dilling	unknown
241 Ramadan Toto	teacher	Dilling	unknown
242 Mosa Babur Khalifa	health worker	El-Khalfan	unknown
243 Jodi Kodin	priest	Heiban	unknown
244 Yousif Kanda Kodi	clerk	Heiban	unknown
245 Daoud Kodi Kodi	teacher	Heiban	unknown
246 Samuel Ali	priest	El-Moro	unknown
247 Salh Takosha	farmer	El-Khalfan	unknown
248 Tawir Basha	retailer	El-Khalfan	unknown
250 Basha Fadle	farmer	Taymeen	unknown
251 El-Sheikh A/Sheikh	sheikh	Taymeen	unknown
252 Yahia Mousa	farmer	Taymeen	unknown
253 Hamid Hassan Damar	retailer	Dilling	unknown
254 Bakri Tulushi	farmer	Tulishi	unknown
255 Willam Tolti	farmer	Tulishi	unknown
256 Ali Mandani	shepherd	Tulishi	unknown
257 Abass El-Yas	health inspector	Dilling	unknown
258 Ali Jubara	farmer	Atoro	unknown
259 Mohamed Kodi	farmer	Kawalib	unknown
260 Sayed Barashot	farmer	Al-Shawaya	unknown
261 Abass Nimir	workman	Nimang /Dilling	unknown
262 Siddik Nimir	shepherd	Nimang /Dilling	unknown
263 Khamis Nimir	policeman	Nimang /Dilling	unknown
264 Salih Nimir	student	Nimang /Dilling	unknown
265 Ibrahim Wina	farmer	Nimang /Dilling	unknown
266 Aradaib Tayar Tofa	farmer	Nimang /Dilling	unknown
267 A/khalil Hussein	tailor	El-Khalfan	unknown
268 Abaker Daldoum	retired	El-Khalfan	unknown
269 Hassan Akan	student	El-Khalfan	unknown

270 Jumma Ejor	farmer	El-Khalfan	unknown
271 Ismail El-doud	med.assistant	Kadugli	unknown
272 Osman Jar el-Nabi	retailer	Nimang /Dilling	unknown
273 Mohamed Atoz Log	worker	Nimang /Dilling	unknown
274 El-Sultan Medeni	Sultan of Tulishi	Tulishi	unknown
275 Mosa Yagoub	student	El-Moro	unknown
276 Bernya Ibra	shepherd	El-Moro	unknown
277 Abdulla Moro	farmer	Kawalib	unknown
278 Khamis Mohamed Eisa	teacher	Nimang /Dilling	unknown
279 Atroun Bilam	retried soldier	Wali /Dilling	unknown
280 Ghabash Hamad	farmer	El-Hadra	unknown
281 Sheikh Mohamed	farmer	El-Hadra	unknown
282 Jumma Murah	driver	El-Khalfan	unknown
283 Ibrahim El-Kabir	driver	El-Khalfan	unknown
284 EL Nour EL Dare	farmer	El-Khalfan	unknown
285 Ebrahim Sulieman	worker	El-Khalfan	unknown
286 Abd El Seid Aman	farmer	Nimang	unknown
287 Ali Khamis	sultan	Kutla	unknown
288 William El Maglis	policeman	El Moro	unknown
289 Hamad Abdulla	retailer	Nimang	unknown
290 Esmail Kabashi	lawyer	Haiban	unknown
291 Jacob El Fiel	clerk	Kawalib	unknown
292 David Kuku (disfigured)	lawyer	El Moro	unknown
293 Kuku Famis	farmer	Fama	unknown
294 Koya Toto	farmer	Fama	unknown
295 Tia Kuwa Rahal	farmer	Fama	unknown
296 Sudani Koko (Kuwin)	farmer	Fama	unknown
297 Kafi Salim	farmer	Fama	unknown
298 Koko Muri	farmer	Fama	unknown
299 Taftish Kafi Shawal	farmer	Fama	unknown
300 Koko Dogmas	wrestler	Fama	unknown
301 Koko Kafi	wrestler	Fama	unknown
302 Tomshala Kuku	farmer	Fama	unknown
303 Kafi Dogmas	farmer	Fama	unknown
304 Hassan Kushaib	retailer	Fama	unknown
305 Koko Abbas	farmer	Fama	unknown
306 Damirgai Tia	farmer	Fama	unknown
307 El Matwa Kuku	farmer	Fama	unknown
308 Tia Kosirgin	farmer	Fama	unknown

1 DPW: Department of Public Works
2 UWA: Underground Water Authority
3 CEC: Central Electricity Company
4 NMAC: Nuba Mountains Agricultural Corporation
5 KTTU: Kadugul Teachers' Trade Union

Information on Contributors

Ahmed Ibrahim Diraige is the Chairman of the Sudan Federal Democratic Alliance, and a former governor of Darfur Region, Sudan. He is an economist by training.

Yousif Kuwa Mekki is an SPLA Commander and Governor of South Kordofan. Before the war he was an elected politician, teacher and leader of the underground Komolo movement of the Nuba. He graduated in political science from the University of Khartoum.

Suleiman Musa Rahhal is the founder of NMSA, Chairman of the Trustees of NRRDO and head of the International Nuba Coordination Centre, London. He is a virologist by profession and holds a fellowship of the Institute of Biomedical Laboratory Scientists.

Julie Flint is a freelance journalist, who has travelled many times to the Nuba Mountains, and made the first and finest film on the Nuba plight, 'Sudan's Secret War: The Nuba', (BBC, 1995).

Neroun Phillip Kuku is Executive Director of NRRDO. He is a graduate in economics from the University of Gezira.

Ian Mackie is an agriculturalist who served in the Nuba Mountains during the 1940s, and is author of *Trek into Nuba* (Edinburgh, The Pentland Press, 1994).

George Rodger, who died in 1995, is a famous British photographer, best-known for his war photography (including the first pictures of Belsen concentration camp) and the photographs from his journeys in Africa in the late 1940s.

Ahmed Abdel Rahman Saeed holds a PhD in chemistry from the University of Manchester Institute of Science and Technology. He is a member of NMSA.

David Stewart-Smith is a freelance photojournalist. He travelled in the Nuba Mountains in 1995 and 1998, the first photographer to devote such time to the Nuba since the outbreak of the war.

Alex de Waal is a director of Justice Africa and author of several books, including *Facing Genocide: The Nuba of Sudan* (London, African Rights, 1995, joint with Yoanes Ajawin).

Peter Woodward is a former Professor of Political Science at the University of Reading, UK, and author of numerous books and articles on Sudan, including *Sudan 1898-1989: The Unstable State* (London, Lynne Reiner, 1990).

International Nuba Coordination Centre

The International Nuba Coordination Centre (INCC) is an international centre for research, advocacy, lobbying and awareness raising activities concerning the Nuba people of Sudan, focussing on their human rights situation, their humanitarian plight, and the political uncertainties facing the Nuba people in the future. The INCC coordinates with the Nub Relief, Rehabilitation and Development Organisation (NRRDO) and organisations in the diaspora including the Nuba Mountains Solidarity Abroad (NMSA). It is a centre for information on the Nuba.

    INCC is an impartial institution that does not hesitate to criticise any political or military organisation that infringes on the collective and individual rights of the Nuba people. It advocates the right of self-determination for the Nuba people and calls for genuine regional autonomy and democracy in the Nuba Mountains. It seeks to end the abuses of human rights suffered by the Nuba, the humanitarian suffering to which they are subjected, and to bring a just end to the war that has afflicted them for too long.

    INCC is the publisher of the Nuba journal NAFIR. Working in collaboration with Sudanese and international human rights organisations, lobbying and advocating the Nuba cause, it has become the voice of the Nuba abroad. The organisation will continue to defend the Nuba's collective rights, voice its opposition to the disproportionate force and pogrom launched against the Nuba people, and to redress the balance of injustice and marginalisation the Nuba people face—prime among them, the right to be Nuba to be in the country of their birth.

Suleiman Musa Rahhal

International Nuba Coordination Centre
Windmill Place, Suite 38
2-4 Windmill Lane
Hanwell, Middlesex UB2 4NJ, UK

Tel/Fax: 44 20 8893 5809

email: Suleimanrahhalincc@compuserve.com